# Divine Healing
A Gift from God

John G Lake

Copyright © 2016 GodSounds, Inc.

All rights reserved.

ISBN: 1541296125
ISBN-13: 978-1541296121

For more information on our voiceover services and to see our online store of Christian audiobooks go to **GodSounds.com**

**OTHER BOOKS AVAILABLE BY GODSOUNDS, INC.**

**Ever Increasing Faith**
by Smith Wigglesworth

**Adventures in God**
by John G Lake

**Intimacy with Jesus: Verse by Verse from the Song of Songs**
by Madame Guyon

**Salvation by Faith**
by John Wesley

**Finney Gold: Words that Helped Birth Revival**
by Charles Finney

**Faith that Prevails**
by Smith Wigglesworth

**Sinners Bound to Change Their Own Hearts**
by Charles Finney

The publishing of this wonderful piece of literature is dedicated to those men and women of God that were not afraid to believe for the impossible.

# TABLE OF CONTENTS

Preface .................................................................... 1
Divine Healing is Not New ..................................... 3
The Science of Divine Healing ........................... 23
Divine Healing ..................................................... 41
The Grace of Divine Healing .............................. 57
Behold, I Give You Power ................................... 63
The Truth About Divine Healing ....................... 73

Jesus Christ was, is, and will always be the healer of man.
Whether we believe it or not.

# PREFACE

GOD HAS GIVEN MAN an amazing body - we are able to fight diseases and recover from physical injury naturally. Over the course of generations, we are able to adjust to certain climates and living situations, which would be difficult for new comers to be exposed to. Our anatomy is a continuous topic of study for scientists; but is all of our healing wrapped up in our physical bodies or in the tools/medicines of doctors?

God has also made available to man another amazing gift – *divine healing*. Such is merely the power of God given to man for the purpose of deliverance from sickness and disease. It is a power originating outside the natural world we live in and derived from the immense glory of the Eternal King.

As Jesus walked the earth, He exhibited the healing power of God. All that came to Jesus received healing. We read no where in Scripture that Jesus could not heal a person afflicted, or refused those that came to him, healing and deliverance. "...He went about doing good, healing all those oppressed by the devil" (Acts 10:38).

I tell you friends, divine healing is available to the Christian soul, whether for personal use or for the purpose of ministry. The same God that healed in the days of Jesus' earthly ministry, is here with us today. We need only to believe and not doubt. We must but trust in the Sacred Scriptures and receive all that God has for us.

I challenge you friends, by the name of Christ Jesus, as you read this amazing book of wisdom and testimonies, seek the Lord of lords for such power. Not so that you may glory in yourself, but so that you can be even as Jesus was. We are all called to imitate God, so why not imitate Him in the sphere of divine healing? Because as many have said before, "Like Father, like Son."

Blessings to you and glory to Jesus Christ our Lord.

**William Crockett**
President of GodSounds, Inc.

## CHAPTER 1

# DIVINE HEALING IS NOT NEW

BELOVED, I FEEL a personal responsibility in speaking to you on the subject of divine healing. This truth was very little known and still less understood prior to the arrival of Brother Tom Hezmalhalch and myself upon these shores, in connection with the introduction and the establishment of the Apostolic Faith Mission in this land.

We had prayerfully considered this subject on our way from America to this country, and had come to the decision that the present was an opportune time to separate this truth from the dogmas and traditions which bound it, and to send it forth on broader lines in harmony with our conception of the truth as it is revealed to us in the Scriptures.

You will therefore appreciate my feelings as I undertake

to address you tonight on this subject.

It is affirmed by the thoughtless that we teach new doctrines. It is not so, for…Divine Healing Is Not New.

It has come to us through a process of progressive revelation running parallel with man's history and perfected in the vicarious death and suffering of our Lord on Calvary.

In its stages of evolution and development, it finds its illustration and parallel in the baptism of the Holy Ghost, which advances from a revelation from God to man in the patriarchal age to that of God dwelling and abiding with man in the Mosaic age, and reaches its climax in the baptism of the Holy Ghost in the Christian dispensation—which is God in man, whereby man becomes the habitation of God through the Spirit.

In Exodus 15:26, God revealed Himself to the people of Israel under His covenant name of Jehovah-Rapha, or "the Lord that healeth thee."

There at the waters of Marah, after they had escaped from the Egyptians and Egyptian medical practitioners by crossing the Red Sea, God made with them…an Everlasting Covenant.

There he made for them a statute and an ordinance, and there he proved them, and said, "if thou wilt diligently hearken to the voice of the Lord thy God, and wilt do that which is right in his sight, and wilt give ear to his commandments, and keep all his statutes, I will put none of these diseases upon thee, which I have brought upon the Egyptians: for I am the Lord that healeth thee." (Exodus 15:25–26)

The covenants of God are as unchangeable and eternal as Himself. The covenant of divine healing stands today as steadfast and irrevocable as the day it was made by the eternal, immutable God at the waters of Marah. It is writ large upon the pages of Holy Writ. Saints have rejoiced in it; prophets have confirmed it; David, the sweet psalmist of Israel, sang in inspired verse of its validity:

Bless the Lord, O my soul: and all that is within me, bless his holy name. Bless the Lord, O my soul, and forget not all his benefits; who forgiveth all thine iniquities; who healeth all thy diseases (Psalm 103:1–3).

Jesus Christ, who was God manifest in the flesh, demonstrated the perpetuity of that covenant in Himself, "healing all manner of sickness and all manner of disease among the people" (Matthew 4:23); by communicating the power of healing the sick to all believers (see Mark 16:15–17); and through the Holy Ghost, placing "the gifts of healing" (1 Corinthians 12:9) as a perpetual manifestation of His power and presence in the church through all ages.

Jesus Christ, like any great reformer, had a specific mission to fulfill. This was outlined in the inspired words of the prophet Isaiah. (See Isaiah 61:1–2.) In the synagogue at Nazareth, at the beginning of His public ministry, Jesus announced the essential points embraced in that ministry imposed upon Him, and which He said was now being fulfilled. Healing was one of the conspicuous features of that ministry, as we read in the fourth chapter of Luke:

> The Spirit of the Lord is upon me, because he hath anointed me to preach the gospel to the poor; he hath sent me to heal the brokenhearted, to preach deliverance to the captives, and recovering of sight to the blind, to set at liberty them that are bruised, to preach the acceptable year of the Lord. (Luke 4:18–19)

Like a true reformer and the Son of God, He put His mission into immediate effect and practice. How did He do it? Read the fourth chapter of Matthew, and you will see the evolution of the ministry of healing:

> And Jesus went about all Galilee, teaching in their synagogues, and preaching the gospel of the

kingdom, and healing all manner of sickness and
all manner of disease among the people.
(Matthew 4:23)

In the ninth chapter of Luke, we read of the first step taken by our Lord suggestive of the broadening, progressive scope of this ministry of healing, by sending forth...Twelve Other Men with Power to Heal.

Then he called his twelve disciples together,
and gave them power and authority over all devils,
and to cure diseases. And he sent them to preach
the kingdom of God, and to heal the sick. (Luke
9:1–2)

And He said unto them, "Take a thousand pounds a year." Is that it? [Voices: No!] Then what is it?
And he said unto them, take nothing for your journey, neither staves, not scrip, neither bread, neither money; neither have two coats apiece.(verse 3)
Oh, my! That is not much like your modern preachers! Today it means the finest house in town, the highest salary, the smartest carriage and horses! Everybody bows down before this display of so much worldly pomp and temporal greatness! These are some of the reasons why the church has lost spiritual power and stands impotent in the presence of sickness and suffering. To hide her feebleness and inefficiency, she takes refuge under the discreditable subterfuge that the gifts of healing have been withdrawn and the age of miracles is past. No wonder infidelity is eating the heart out of the church of God! Has Jehovah-Rapha, the eternal covenant God, changed? Or, is the modern disciple of a different stamp and pattern than they whom Jesus called in the days of His flesh? Truly, the change is in the disciple and not in the one unchangeable Lord and Master. I find that the old-time power is to be had today by the old-time men who are willing to walk and

work and suffer and die to get this gospel of Christ to people everywhere.

He endued the twelve with the power. And in the tenth chapter of Luke we read how the Lord took an additional step to the extension of the scope of the ministry of divine healing by sending forth...Seventy More Men with the Power to Heal.

"After these things the Lord appointed other seventy also" (Luke 10:1); and in verse 9 we read that Jesus commanded them to "heal the sick that are therein, and say unto them, the kingdom of God is come nigh unto you." There were now eighty-three men endued with this power: Christ Himself, the twelve disciples, and the seventy more. At the close of the forty days separating the event of the crucifixion from that of the ascension, our Lord still further extends the range of the ministry of healing by furnishing...Every Believer with the Power to Heal the Sick.

Every person, in every age, in every land, who has faith in the living, eternal, covenant-keeping God is empowered to lay hands upon the sick, and "they shall recover" (Mark 16:18). The general terms of that great extension of the ministry of healing are found in that great and final commission given in Matthew 28: "And Jesus came and spake unto them, saying, all power is given unto me in heaven and in earth" (verse 18).

Beloved, has He lost any of that power? Never! He is still the Son of God.

All power is given unto me in heaven and in earth. Go ye therefore, and teach all nations, baptizing them in the name of the Father, and of the Son, and of the Holy Ghost: teaching them to observe all things whatsoever I have commanded you: and, lo, I am with you alway, even unto the end of the world.(Matthew 28:18–20)

Is He with us still? Yes, bless God. Is He changed? No. "Jesus Christ the same yesterday, and to day, and for ever" (Hebrews 13:8). "I am the Lord, I change not" (Malachi

3:6). "For the gifts and calling of God are without repentance" (Romans 11:29). God has never repented of having placed the gifts of the Holy Ghost in the church. In the name of Jesus Christ, I challenge any man to show by the Word of God that the gifts and power of God were withdrawn. We have lost the old-time faith—that is where the trouble is! Having forsaken God to lean upon the arms of flesh, and the fountain of living waters for broken cisterns that can hold no water (see Jeremiah 2:13), let us honestly acknowledge our sin and return to the Lord our God.

Having examined the general terms of that extension of the ministry of healing, let us now consider the peculiar characteristic, the trademark of God's endorsement, which was to be the accompanying circumstance, the continuous sign and symbol of the gospel of Jesus Christ. This is given in the sixteenth chapter of Mark:

> Afterward he appeared unto the eleven as they sat at meat, and upbraided them with their unbelief and hardness of heart, because they believed not them which had seen him after he was risen. And he said unto them, "Go ye into all the world, and preach the gospel to every creature. He that believeth and is baptized shall be saved; but he that believeth not shall be damned. And these signs shall follow them that believe; in my name shall they cast out devils; they shall speak with new tongues; they shall take up serpents; and if they drink any deadly thing, it shall not hurt them; they shall lay hands on the sick, and they shall recover." (Mark 16:14–18)

"And these signs." These are God's own mark and endorsement of the faithful preaching of the gospel of Jesus Christ. We know the goods by the trademark that they beat. These signs are God's eternal trademark, issued by the Son of God, and sealed in His own blood. The devil has tried to rob us of it by telling the preachers and teachers that these verses are an interpolation, and not found in the Sinaitic manuscript of the New Testament. The Sinaitic manuscript was, however, only written in the fourth century. That these verses are authentic has been proved from the writings of the church fathers, which were written prior to the Sinaitic manuscript, and less than two hundred and seventy years after Christ.

This is a matter of history. Lord Hailes, an eighteenth century Scottish writer, is our authority. He tells us that at a dinner at Edinburgh, it was decided that a compilation of the New Testament be made from the New Testament references and quotations found in the writings of the church fathers, previous to ad 300. The whole was completed some years ago and found identical with our present edition, except that it lacked seven verses in Hebrews, and these have since been forthcoming. Preachers and teachers of God's Word, don't make any more infidels with such an excuse, but rather confess that the faith to get results is lacking, that the Word is true, that the failure is on the human side.

Have you noticed how frequently church officers and members say, "Oh, I don't believe this or that portion of God's Word!" Why don't they? How could they when the Word of God is continually twisted out of its original sense and meaning by those whose vocation should be to guard it as a sacred deposit? This wresting of the Scriptures is responsible for the unwarranted belief that the gifts of the Holy Ghost have been withdrawn.

Jesus said, "These signs shall follow [not the doubter, but] them that believe; in my name [the name of Jesus] shall they cast out devils; they shall speak with new tongues; they shall take up serpents; and if they drink any deadly thing, it shall not hurt them; they shall lay hands on the sick, and they shall recover."

Someone asks, "What does it mean to cast out devils?"

It means that the man with the Holy Ghost dwelling within him is the master and has dominion over every devilish force and counterfeit. At Johannesburg, someone said, "Your power is hypnotism." One night, God demonstrated through us the falsity of that accusation. The power that is within the true Christian is the power of the living Christ, and "greater is he that is in you, than he that is in the world" (1 John 4:4).

I can best illustrate this by introducing an incident in my own personal ministry.

## THE POWER OF GOD AGAINST HYPNOTISM

In the Johannesburg Tabernacle, at a Sunday evening service about a year ago, God instantly healed a lame girl. She came from Germiston. She had been suffering for three-and-a-half years from what the doctors said was either an extreme case of rheumatism or the first stage of hip disease. She was not able to get up the steps without assistance when she came to the platform to be prayed for. They asked her, "How long have you been sick?"

She said, "For three-and-a-half years."

"Have the doctors treated you?"

"Yes; for two-and-a-half years, and then they gave me up."

"Who has been treating you for the last year?"

"A hypnotist."

Just then, a well-known hypnotist arose in the audience and moved forward and took the front seat. The leader said, "Never mind about the hypnotist; Jesus is going to heal you right now. In two minutes you will be well." They laid hands on her and prayed, and instantly the Lord delivered her, and she walked up and down the platform several times to demonstrate to herself and the audience that she was well.

The leader said:

> I stepped back and looked at her, my heart going out in praise to God for His mercy, when suddenly the Spirit of the Lord descended upon me in power—not in any gentle influence, but with a mighty intense power—a spirit of revulsion against the spirit in the hypnotist. I stepped on the platform directly in front of him and said, "Are you the man who has been hypnotizing this woman?"
> 
> He replied, "Yes, I am." He rose to his feet and looked towards me in a challenging attitude.
> 
> I said to him, "In the name of Jesus Christ, you will never hypnotize anybody again." And before I realized what I was doing, I reached over the front of the platform, grasped his collar with my left hand, while with my right I slapped him on the back, saying, "In the name of Jesus Christ, the Son of God, you come out of him now." I said, "go and hypnotize another if you can."
> 
> He laughed at me and said, "Do you mean to tell me that I cannot hypnotize anybody?"
> 
> I said, "Yes, sir, that is the end of the thing. The devil that caused you to hypnotize people is out."
> 
> He worked all night in an endeavor to hypnotize some subjects, and in the morning at six came to my house saying, "This is a mighty serious business, mister, this is my bread and butter." He wanted me to give him back the

power to hypnotize.

I explained to him that it was not I but Jesus who had cast out the devil. I added, "Brother, it looks to me as if the Lord wanted you to earn an honest living."

He cancelled his engagement at the theatre where he was billed to give exhibitions, and last heard of, he was working in the mine and earning an honest living.

That demonstrated there is a mighty manifestation of the Spirit of God that has dominion over every other power. It is still true that in His name we shall cast out devils.

## BROTHER FISHER AND "THEY SHALL TAKE UP SERPENTS"

This afternoon I heard a brother ask, "What about 'They shall take up serpents?'" Let me tell you a story. Brother Fisher of Los Angeles, California, told me this incident in his own life. He was a Baptist minister at Glendale, a suburb of Los Angeles.

One morning my wife called me up on the telephone and said the water pipe beneath the house was broken. I went home about ten in the morning. I opened the little door in the basement of the house and, on putting my hand in to feel for the pipe, I was bitten by a serpent. At once I commenced to swell. The poison worked into my body fast. What was I to do? I said, "God, Your Word says, 'They shall take up serpents.' I trust You for this; You must heal me or I die."

That afternoon and evening my sufferings were terrible. By midnight my blood was so congealed I was well nigh insensible. Oh, I shall never forget that sense of death creeping over me, steadily, surely, until three in the morning. I could pray no more. I ceased to struggle, I fell to the floor, and that instant God healed me. The life of God thrilled through my body, and I was healed. It is true, "They shall take up serpents."

## BROTHER TOM AND "THEY SHALL TAKE UP SERPENTS"

Let me give you another illustration of "taking up serpents." It is an event in the life of Brother Tom Hezmalhalch, one of the pastors of the Apostolic Faith Mission in Johannesburg. Brother Tom, as we call him for short, is a man of great faith and simple trust in God. (He has since returned to America.)

> In Southern California, during one of the harvest seasons, I had an honest young infidel working for me. The young man was engaged in loading, and I was pitching sheaves on the load, when he said, 'Brother Tom, do you believe in the Bible?'
> 
> I said, "Every word of it."
> 
> He said, "Do you believe in Mark 16:18?"
> 
> I said, "I do."
> 
> He answered, "I have never yet met the person who does."
> 
> I prayed silently to Jesus, that if He wanted to convince this young man of the truth of His Word, that He send along a snake, and I would take it up. Soon I heard a hissing sound from under the sheaves. I said, "Jesus sent you along; I

want you." I grabbed the snake some distance from the head, and I lifted it up to my friend on the wagon. He looked at me and then said, "Kill it! Kill it!"

"No," I said, "Jesus sent it along; I am going to let it go about its own business."

After a while he laughed, and said, "Tom, that was only a common Californian snake."

I judged from his expression he was not satisfied with the test. I prayed again. "Jesus, why did You send along a common snake? If you want to convince this man, send along a venomous one."

Not long after, I heard the hiss of another snake. I cried, "Hold on there; I want you," and laying hold of it as I did the former one, I held it up to my friend, saying, "How about Mark 16:18?"

He turned pale and said hastily, "Drop it! Drop it! Kill it."

I put it quietly down after stroking its head and body with my other hand, and said, "Go on, Jesus sent you here, I'll not kill you."

When my friend could speak, for he was pale and shocked, he said, "Tom, did you know what kind of a snake that was?"

I said, "No."

He replied, "That was a deadly viper, and if it had bitten you, you would be a dead man."

I said, "It could not bite. Jesus would not permit it."

I don't pretend to have that kind of faith, but I am not going to belittle it in the man who has. I am, I trust, man and Christian enough to praise God when I see someone going further than I can.

## "IF THEY DRINK ANY DEADLY THING, IT SHALL NOT HURT THEM"

You ask, "What about, 'If they drink any deadly thing, it shall not hurt them?'" History abounds with instances in which the early Christians were compelled to drink the juice of the deadly hemlock, but through faith in Jesus, one of the deadliest of poisons became as harmless as water. According to your faith be it done unto you. (See Matthew 9:29.)

My own sister's son, Fred Moffatt, when a child, entered his father's workshop and ate some Paris green. My sister and brother-in-law sent for me. I quoted the words of our Savior, "And if they drink any deadly thing, it shall not hurt them." Upon this precious promise of God we rested, and Jesus healed the child. (His parents now reside at 4 Milbourn Road, Bertrams, Johannesburg, and their son was a student at the Marist Brothers Schools and has since returned to America.)

•

I have outlined the development and progressive revelation of divine healing from the covenant at Marah, and on through succeeding dispensations until it is perfected in the redemption wrought by Christ on Calvary. The blessings of healing in the old as well as the new dispensation flow from the atonement that Jesus Christ, the Son of God, made for man's sin and sickness on the cross of Calvary.

In Matthew, we read:

> He cast out the spirits with his word, and healed all that were sick: that it might be fulfilled which was spoken by Esaias the prophet, saying,

"Himself took our infirmities, and bare our sicknesses." (Matthew 8:16–17)

In the general epistle of James, through the inspired writer, the Holy Ghost instructs the Christian what to do when sick.

Is any sick among you? Let him call for the elders of the church; and let them pray over him, anointing him with oil in the name of the Lord: and the prayer of faith shall save the sick, and the Lord shall raise him up; and if he hath committed sins, they shall be forgiven him."
(James 5:14–15)

In spite of the clear, convincing testimony of the Scriptures and the ever accumulating cloud of witnesses who testify of healing received through faith in Jesus, many preachers and teachers are still found blindly rejecting the truth to their own final discomfiture and undoing.

## GOD HAS A CONTROVERSY WITH THE CHURCH IN AFRICA

Your own prophet, the Reverend Andrew Murray, was healed of God at Bethshan, London, England, of a throat disease that medical skill had proved itself impotent to heal. Thirty years ago the reverend gentleman wrote a book containing the fundamental teaching on divine healing. Why was it withdrawn from circulation? Why is it not possible to obtain this book at any of the Christian literature depots in Africa?

Why? Because the preachers foresaw that the members of their churches would call upon them for the exercise of that faith which saves the sick! They feared the ordeal which would test their faith in God and the value of their own prayers! Instead of confessing their spiritual poverty and inefficiency and reaching out to touch the springs of life and power in God, they fell back into a state of even greater spiritual apathy and inertness, being satisfied with the cold externals of religious forms and observances, which without the indwelling life-giving power and presence of the Holy Ghost have no saving grace or spiritual virtue.

## DIVINE HEALING IS THE SEAL OF GOD'S ACKNOWLEDGMENT

Divine healing is the seal of God's acknowledgment and the proof to the world that Jesus Christ is the Son of God. John the Baptist was in prison. He was troubled with doubts as to whether Jesus was the Christ. He sent two of his disciples to Jesus to put the question, "Art thou he that should come, or do we look for another?" (Matthew 11:3). Jesus' answer was to appeal to the signs of His ministry. These were, and are still, God's answer to doubt or unbelief:

> Go and show John again these things which ye do hear and see: The blind receive their sight, and the lame walk, and the lepers are cleansed, and the deaf hear, the dead are raised up, and the poor have the gospel preached to them. And blessed is he, whosoever shall not be offended in me. (Matthew 11:4–6)

These are still God's seal and endorsement of the preaching of the true gospel. The preaching that lacks the signs that Jesus promised lacks the divine attestation by which God confirms the preaching of as own true gospel. "Take heed, brethren, lest there be in any of you an evil heart of unbelief, in departing from the living God"

(Hebrews 3:12).

And at the end of the age as at the beginning, the command of Jesus Christ to all workers everywhere is:

> Go ye into all the world, and preach the gospel to every creature. He that believeth and is baptized shall be saved; but he that believeth not shall be damned. And these signs shall follow them that believe; In my name shall they cast out devils; they shall speak with new tongues; they shall take up serpents; and if they drink any deadly thing, it shall not hurt them; they shall lay hands on the sick, and they shall recover. (Mark 16:15–18)

The results now, as then, will be, "And they went forth, and preached every where, the Lord working with them, and confirming the word with signs following." (Mark 16:20).

## MY GRACE IS SUFFICIENT FOR THEE

> The other evening I was riding home after a heavy day's work; I felt very wearied, and sore depressed, when swiftly, and suddenly as a lightning flash, that text came to me: "My grace is sufficient for thee" (2 Corinthians 12:9). I reached home and looked it up in the original, and at last it came to me in this way: "My grace is sufficient for thee." I said, "I should think it is, Lord," and burst out laughing. I never fully understood what the holy laughter of Abraham was until then. It seemed to make unbelief so absurd. It was as though some little fish, being very thirsty, was troubled about drinking the river dry, and Father Thames said, "Drink away, little fish, my stream is

sufficient for thee."

Or, it seemed like a little mouse in the granaries of Egypt, after the seven years of plenty, fearing it might die of famine. Joseph might say, "Cheer up, little mouse, my granaries are sufficient for thee." Again, I imagined a man away up yonder, in a lofty mountain, saying to himself, "I breathe so many cubic feet of air every year; I fear I shall exhaust the oxygen in the atmosphere." But the earth might say, "Breathe away, O man, and fill thy lungs ever, my atmosphere is sufficient for thee." Oh, brethren, be great believers! Little faith will bring your souls to heaven, but great faith will bring heaven to your souls.
—Charles H. Spurgeon

They shall be abundantly satisfied with the fatness of thy house; and thou shalt make them drink of the river of thy pleasures. (Psalm 36:8)

I am come that they might have life, and that they might have it more abundantly. (John 10:10)

But my God shall supply all your need, according to his riches in glory by Christ Jesus. (Philippians 4:19)

Jehovah fills to the brim the vessels faith presents to Him.

The present circumstance, which presses so hard against you, if surrendered to Christ, is the shaped tool in the Father's hand to chisel you for eternity. Trust Him then. Do not push away the instrument lest you lose its work.

## A NICKEL FOR THE LORD

Yesterday he wore a rose on the lapel of his coat, but when the plate was passed today, he gave a nickel to the Lord. He had several bills in his pocket and sundry change, perhaps a dollar's worth, but he hunted about, and finding this poor little nickel, he laid it on the plate to aid the church militant in its fight against the world, the flesh, and the devil. His silk hat was beneath the seat, and his gloves and cane were beside it, and the nickel was on the plate—a whole nickel.

On Saturday afternoon he met a friend, and together they had some refreshments. The cash register stamped thirty-five cents on the slip the boy presented to him. Peeling off a bill he handed it to the lad and gave him a nickel tip when he brought back the change. A nickel for the Lord and a nickel for the waiter.

And the man had his shoes polished on Saturday afternoon and handed out a dime without a murmur. He had a shave and paid fifteen cents with equal alacrity. He took a box of candies home to his wife and paid forty cents for them, and the box was tied with a dainty bit of ribbon. Yes, and he also gave a nickel to the Lord.

Who is this Lord? Who is He? Why, the man worships Him as Creator of the universe, the One who puts the stars in order, and by whose immutable decree the heavens stand. Yes, he does, and he dropped a nickel in to support the church militant.

And what is the church militant?

The church militant is the church that represents upon the earth the triumphant church of the great God.

And the man knew that he was an atom in space, and he knew that the almighty was without limitations, and knowing this he put his hand in his pocket, and picked out the nickel, and gave it to the Lord.

And the Lord being gracious, and slow to anger, and knowing our frame, did not slay the man for the meanness of his offering but gives him this day his daily bread.

But the nickel was ashamed, if the man was not.

The nickel hid beneath a quarter that was given by a poor woman who washes for a living.

JOHN G LAKE

CHAPTER 2

# THE SCIENCE OF DIVINE HEALING

OUR EYES BEHOLD THE TRIUMPH of Jesus Christ, the glorious and victorious Son of God, who triumphed over death and hell; who arose triumphant, salvation to obtain; that we might behold gladness and joy, and walk triumphant through Jesus Christ, through the blood that washes "whiter than snow" (Psalm 51:7).

"In him was life; and the life was the light of men" (John 1:4). This Scripture reveals the difference between Christianity and philosophy. Some are inquiring why it is that there is always that keynote in my addresses.

God gave me the privilege of intimacy with the philosophic East, where multitudes are ministered to by Buddhist, Confucianist, and Brahman priests. Every cult imaginable has its representatives there. I was amazed to discover that many in the Western world were gradually assimilating the philosophies of the East.

When you take the modern philosophies—Christian Science, New Thought, Unity, Divine Science, etc.—today and examine them, you discover that they are the same old philosophies of India, Egypt, and China from time immemorial. They were constructed before the Redeemer came, so there is no redemption in them. They are an endeavor to redeem one's self through self-effort.

As I said before, the difference between philosophy and religion, particularly the religion of Jesus Christ, is in the words I quoted from the Scriptures: "In him was life, and the life was the light of men." Philosophy is light; it is the best light the individual possessed who framed the philosophy, but it is not a life giver.

But from the soul of Jesus there breathed a holy life of God that comes into the nature of man, quickens him by its power, and by the grace of God, he has the life of Jesus in him, eternal light, eternal life. Bless God.

Many of the ancient philosophies have light. It is said by some writers that one of the Indian philosophies, the Bhagavad Gita, was written eight hundred years before Isaiah. It predicts the coming of Krishna, a son of God, not the Son of God. Listen to this philosophic jewel:

Never the spirit was born.
The spirit shall cease to be never.
Never was time it was not.
End and beginning are dreams.
Birthless and deathless and changeless
Remaineth the spirit forever;
Death hath not changed it at all,
Dead though the house of it seems.

Yet no knowledge of redemption and no knowledge of a redeemer is there.

Buddha presented his philosophy five hundred years

before Jesus. The philosophies of Egypt tell the story of the flood and were written thousands of years before Jesus Christ. In the writings of each one of them, you will find many of the teachings of Jesus. The teachings of Jesus were not unique in that they were new; rather, they were new in that they contained something that none of the rest possessed. It was the divine content in the Word of Jesus Christ that gave His teachings their distinguishing feature from the other philosophies. That content is the life of God. "In him was life, and the life was the light of men."

The philosophies were man's best endeavor to find an explanation of life. Without knowledge of a redeemer, they were written before Christ was manifest in the world. Their authors denied the power of sin or nullified its influence as they failed to conceive of a redeeming grace, an in-working of God in man, through the Spirit of Christ, to save from sin's power and change his nature. But there is given unto us "exceeding great and precious promises: that by these ye might be partakers of the divine nature" (2 Peter 1:4).

Beloved, the real Christian, and the real Christian church, undertakes to bring to mankind the life of the Lord Jesus, knowing that when the life of Jesus comes, the illumination of the soul, the light of civilization, and Christianity will follow, but the life is first.

As men wandered from God, and as the world neglected God, men naturally fell into their own consciousness and soul states and proceeded in the common way of the world to endeavor to bless the world through light—but light never saved a world. Light never will save a world. There must be a divine content from on high that comes to the soul to enrich it and to empower it, to illuminate it and to glorify it, and more, to deify it. For God's purpose through Jesus Christ is to deify the nature of man and thus forever make him like unto Christ, not only in his outward appearance and habits of life, but in nature and substance and content, in spirit and soul and body, like the Son of God.

Jesus never intended Christians to be an imitation. They were to be bone of His bone and blood of His blood and flesh of His flesh and soul of His soul and spirit of His Spirit. And thus, He becomes to us Son of God, Savior and Redeemer forever, and we are made one with Him both in purpose and being.

Interpretation of a Message in Tongues:

> Our Father God, to Thee we give the praise of our hearts, that by Thy grace we have been privileged to live in a world where not only the light of God was known, but where the life of God has come. We bless Thee that we have the privilege of living in a day when the life of God in a new flood of power and glory from heaven is coming upon a city and parched and barren world. And we thank Thee that this life of God has been in our hearts the holy water of life, blessing and enriching our nature, filling us with Thy divine grace and power through Jesus Christ the Lord.

Throughout my life, a spirit of investigation predominated. It has never been easy to accept truth readily, until my soul stepped out inch by inch and proved the ground. When approaching this matter of baptism of the Spirit it was with great care, but as a hungry soul. My heart was hungry for God. And one day the Spirit of the Lord came upon me, God flooded my life and baptized me in His Holy Spirit, and then a new and powerful working of God began in my heart which has gone on for fifteen years, until Christ has become in my world a divine reality.

Having formal acknowledgment as a student of science, it is my privilege to attend clinics, which I frequently do. I submitted myself at one time to a series of experiments. It was not sufficient to know that God healed; I had to know how God healed. I visited one of the great experimental institutions and submitted myself for a series of experiments.

First, they attached to my head an instrument to record the vibrations of the brain. This instrument had an indicator that would register the vibrations of the mind. So I began by repeating soothing things like the Twenty-third Psalm, calculated to soothe the mind and reduce its vibrations to the lowest point. Then I repeated the Thirty-seventh Psalm, then the thirty-fifth [chapter] of Isaiah, then the Ninety-first Psalm, then Paul's address before Agrippa. After this, I went into secular literature and recited Tennyson's "Charge of the Light Brigade" and last, Poe's "The Raven," with a prayer in my heart that at the psychological moment, God would anoint my soul in the Holy Ghost.

My difficulty was that while the reciting went on, I could not keep the Spirit from coming upon me, and when I got through with Poe's "The Raven," they said, "You are a phenomenon. You have a wider mental range than any human being we have ever seen." In reality that was not so. It was because the Spirit of God kept coming upon me in degree, so I could feel the moving of the Spirit within me.

But I prayed in my heart, Lord God, if You will only let the Spirit of God come like the lightnings of God upon my soul for two seconds, I know something is going to happen that these men have never seen before.

So, as I closed the last lines, suddenly the Spirit of God struck me in a burst of praise and tongues, and the old indicator on the instrument bounced to its limit, and I haven't the least idea how much further it would have gone if it were a possibility. The professors said, "We have never seen anything like it."

I replied, "Gentlemen, it is the Holy Ghost."

Now, in order to get the force of this lesson, it is necessary to give you the latest theory of the process of digestion. You will see the assimilating power of your nature, your capacity to assimilate God and take the life of God into your being and keep it in your being. I am not talking about what I believe; I am talking about what I know.

For many years God kept me so that sickness and death could not touch me, from the day that I saw in the ninety-first Psalm a man's privilege of entering into God, not only for healing, but also for health and having God and the life of God in every fiber of his being.

Scientists tell us that in a single inch of a man's skin there are one million, five hundred thousand cells, and they have almost doubled that statement now. But be that as it may, the whole structure of a man's being is one wonderful cellular structure. Your blood, your body, your brain, your bone is just one great cellular structure.

According to the latest theory on the process of digestion, the food we eat is reduced to vegetable lymph and is then absorbed into the body cells. But no scientist in the world has ever been able to satisfactorily explain what it is that changes the lymph and makes it life. Something happens when it is in the cells that changes it to life. This is transmutation.

I want to tell you what grew up in my soul and how I proved the fact. I could feel sometimes while in the attitude of prayer, just as you have felt hundreds of times, the impulse of the Spirit moving through my brain and my person to the tips of my fingers, just little impulses of God's presence in my life. And I said, "If there was an instrument powerful enough, I believe men could see the action of the brain cells and see what takes place."

Here is the secret of digestion: from the spirit-mind of man and through the spirit of man, there is imparted to every cell of your body impulses of spirit, waves of life. It is the movement of the Spirit. Spirit impulses pass from the cortex cells of the brain to the very ends of your fingers and toes, to every cell of the body. And when they touch that vegetable lymph in the body cells, it is transformed into life. That is transmutation.

In the electrical world you can dissolve zinc, and the electrical current absorbs it and transmits it to the other end of the wire. In an experiment in California, they dissolved zinc in the battery at the one end, transmitted the zinc to the other end of the wire, and deposited and solidified it at the other end of the wire, a distance of twelve miles. How is it done? There is a process of transmutation. That is what it is called. It is a change from one form to another.

My brother, listen. If that is not true in the spiritual world, there is no such thing as divine life; there is no such thing as salvation through the Son of God, for that which is soulish or natural must be transformed by the Spirit of God in us until it becomes spiritual—until it is of God. "Ye must be born again" (John 3:7) is a truly scientific statement.

Jesus sat with His disciples and ate with them, both bread and fish. He went to the Mount and ascended before them to glory, while their eyes beheld. What happened to the fish and the bread that He had eaten? I tell you there is transmutation. That which is natural becomes spiritual. That which was natural was changed by the power of God into the life of God, into the nature of God, into the substance of God, into the glory of God.

In the second experiment, they attached to my head a powerful X-ray with microscopic attachments in order to see, if possible, what the action of the brain cells were. Then I proceeded, just as in the former experiment. First, I repeated Scriptures that were soothing and calculated to reduce the action of the cortex cells to their lowest possible register. Then, I went on into the Scriptures to the better and richer things, until I came to the first of John; and as I began to recite that and the fires of God began to burn in my heart, presently, once again the Spirit of God came upon me, and the man who was at my back touched me. It was a signal to keep the poise of soul until one after another could look through the instrument. And finally when I let go, the Spirit subsided. They said, "Why, man, we cannot understand this, but the cortex cells expanded amazingly."

Oh, beloved, when you pray, something is happening in you. It is not a myth; it is the action of God. The almighty God, by the Spirit, comes into the soul, takes possession of the brain, manifests in the cortex cells, and when you will and wish (either consciously or unconsciously) the fire of God, the power of God, that life of God, that nature of God, is transmitted from the cortex cells of the brain, throbs through your nerves, down through your person, into every cell of your being, into every cell of your brain and blood and flesh and bone, into the million, five hundred thousand cells in every square inch of your skin, and they are alive with God. That is divine healing.

Men have treated the gospel of Jesus Christ as though it were a sentiment and foolishness. Men who posed as being wise have scorned the phenomenon taking place in the Christian every day. But beloved, no dear old mother ever knelt before the throne of God and raised her heart to heaven without demonstrating the finest process of divine wireless transmission.

In these days, they are now able to transmit by wireless from six to seven thousand miles and even twelve thousand miles recently. Once again, they have been able to demonstrate that in one-tenth of a second they can transmit the first section of thought twelve thousand miles. Think of it! There is practically no such thing as time; it is practically done instantaneously. This explains instantaneous salvation and instantaneous healing.

Beloved, the very instant your soul moves with your heart cry and your nature yearns after God, it registers in the soul of Jesus Christ, and the answer comes back. So Jesus said, "What things soever ye desire, when ye pray, believe that ye receive them, and ye shall have them" (Mark 11:24), and "While [ye] are yet speaking, I will hear" (Isaiah 65:24).

I said to them, "Gentlemen, I want you to see one more thing. You go down in your hospital and bring the man who has inflammation in the shinbone. Take your instrument and attach it to his leg; leave space enough to get my hand on his leg. You can have it attached on both sides." So when the instrument was all ready, I put my hand on that man's shin, and I prayed just like Mother Etter prays, just as you all pray. No strange prayer, but the cry of my heart to God. I said, "God, kill the devilish disease by the power of God. Let the Spirit live in him; let it move in him."

Then I said, "Gentlemen, what is taking place?"

They replied, "Every cell is responding."

Beloved, all there is to healing is that the life of God comes back into the part that is afflicted, and right away the blood flows, the congested cells respond, and the work is done. That is again God's divine science in healing.

My soul long ago grew tired of men treating the whole subject of Christianity as though it were child's play. We have our physical sciences; we have our psychological sciences, the structure of the body and the action of the mind taught in the great schools of the land. But there is something greater. One of these days there is going to be a new chair in our universities. It will be the chair of pneumatology, the science of spirit, by which men will undertake to discover the laws of the spirit of man and the action of God through man. And by the grace of God, men shall know that God is alive and that the living Spirit of God is no dream; and its wondrous power in man and through man will be revealed.

In my healing rooms in Spokane, a dear woman came one day whose name is Lamphear. She was the wife of a merchant in the city. She had fallen down some stairs, causing a prolapse of the stomach, bowels, and uterus. She had been an invalid for eleven years. On top of this, she became tubercular unto death. On top of that, the poor woman developed inflammatory rheumatism, until she lived in a hell of torture. The physicians said there was nothing they could do for her, but advised that they take her to Soap Lake, Oregon, and perhaps the baths would do her some good.

So they put her in the hot baths there, and she suffered just as much as ever. Then they tried super-heated baths, and they put her in water hotter than any human being had ever been in before—so the superintendent testified. The result was that instead of having any healing effect, the left leg developed an abnormal growth, and it became three inches longer than the other leg, and a bone spur larger than an orange grew on the inside of the knee, destroying the action of the knee joint. The foot became an inch longer.

She came away from the institution worse than she went. She got as far as Portland. Her parents were living at The Dalles. She wanted to see her patents before she died, so her husband carried her in his arms to the boat. As he did so, a Pentecostal missionary stepped up and said, "Dear woman, we understand now why God told us to take this boat. He told us last night to take the eight o'clock boat for The Dalles." He called up on the telephone and found that the fare was $1.80, and as that was all the money they had, they went without their breakfast so as to be able to take the boat.

As she lay crying with her suffering (they were timid folks), the man said, "When we get to The Dalles, we will pray for you." Eventually, they reached The Dalles and went to a hotel. The two knelt to pray for her, and she says that as they prayed and put their hands on her knees, that their hands became illuminated until they looked like the hands of Jesus, their faces looked like the face of Jesus, and she was afraid. But something happened. The pain went out of her.

Strangely, she retained her tuberculosis, and the struggle for breath went on. The leg remained the same length. When she examined herself, she was surprised to discover that it was not shorter. She said, "Pray again that the Lord may make it the same length as the other," but the poor missionary was staggered.

He said, "Dear Sister, the pain is gone, you should be satisfied and give praise to God."

So she went on for three-and-a-half years, coughing her lungs out and her one leg three inches longer than the other. One day she came to the healing rooms and was ministered to. The healing action of God took place, and she felt wonderfully relieved. She said, "I can breathe clear down into my stomach."

The minister said, "What makes you limp?"

She replied, "There is a big lump on the inside of my knee, and my leg is three inches longer than it should be."

He said, "I'll pray for that."

But she said, "The missionary who prayed for me told me I should be satisfied if the pain was gone."

The minister said, "He had not grown up in God yet." And he put his hands on the lump and prayed, and God almighty dissolved that lump of bone and that leg shortened at the rate of one inch a week. The foot also shortened to its proper length, and she wears shoes like anyone else, the same on both feet. She was born without the outer rim and lobe on one ear, and it also grew and became like the other.

There is a difference between healing and miracle. Healing is the restoration of diseased tissue, but miracle is a creative action of the Spirit of God, creating that which is deficient in a man's life. And the salvation of a soul is a divine miracle of God. Every time Christ speaks the word of life to a man's heart, there is a divine, creative miracle of God wrought in him, and he is a new man in Christ Jesus.

One day I sat in Los Angeles, talking to old father Seymour. I told him an incident in the life of Elias

Letwaba, one of our native preachers who lived in the country. I came to his home, and his wife said, "He is not home. A little baby is hurt, and he is praying for it." So we went over, and I got down on my knees and crawled into the native hut. I saw he was kneeling in a corner by the child. I said, "Letwaba, it is me. What is the matter with the child?" He told me that the mother had it on her back in a blanket, as natives carry their children, and it had fallen out. He said, "I think it has hurt its neck."

I examined it and saw that the baby's neck was broken, and I said to Letwaba, "Why, Letwaba, the baby's neck is broken." It would turn like the neck of a doll from side to side. I did not have faith for a broken neck, but poor old Letwaba did not know the difference. I saw he did not understand, but he discerned the spirit of doubt in my soul, and I said to myself, "I am not going to interfere with his faith. He will just feel the doubt generated by the old traditional things I ever learned. So I will go out."

And I did. I went and sat in another hut and kept on praying. I lay down at one a.m.; at three Letwaba came in. I said, "Well, Letwaba, how about the baby?"

He looked at me so lovingly and sweetly and said, "Why brother, the baby is all well. Jesus did heal the baby."

I said, "The baby is well! Letwaba, take me to the baby at once."

So we went to the baby, and I took the little black infant on my arm, and I came out praying, "Lord take every cursed thing out of my soul that keeps me from believing the Lord Jesus Christ." And Mr. Seymour, to whom I had related the incident, shouted, "Praise God, brother, that is not healing, it is life!"

In my meeting in Spokane is a dear man who came from Texas, Reverend Julias Allen. He told us he was dying of pellagra. He came to Sister Etter's meeting at Dallas. On the train he apparently died, and they laid his body in the station house, covered him with gunnysacks, but discovered in the morning that he was still alive. So they carried him to Mother Etter's meeting, and she came down off the platform and prayed for him, rebuking that devil of pellagra. That man is living and has been preaching the gospel for seven years at Spokane.

Why, there is more science in the mind of God in five minutes than the bloated scholarship of the world ever knew. "In Him is life, and the life was the light of men" (John 1:4). The life of God is that which the mind of men and the keenest of them never knew and never understood. "The world by wisdom knew not God" (1 Corinthians 1:21). They could not discern the value in His death or understand the marvels of His life or why the Lord Jesus came and lived and died and entered into Hades and destroyed the power of darkness and death that held the souls of men; or how He liberated them from the chains of darkness, translated them to His own glory, and came forth to speak God's Word and reveal God's power and show God's nature. And by the grace of God, man has been privileged to enter into the nature of Jesus, and the fires of God burn in his soul like they burned in the soul of the risen Lord. That explains resurrection faith and resurrection power.

The scientific world has been startled by one of the English scientists, who says he has a formula for transmutation of the grosser metals into gold. The old alchemists claimed to know this secret, but somehow it disappeared from the world. Now it is claimed it can be done again—that they can take lead and silver and iron and transmute, or change, them into gold.

Beloved, that is the thing that Jesus Christ has been doing all the time. It is as old as Christianity; it is as old as the Son of God. He has been coming to the hearts of men, taking the old base conditions of the nature, injecting His life into them, inducting His power into the man, and through the mighty action of the Holy Ghost, they have been changed into the pure gold of God. That is divine transmutation.

If there never was another blessing that came to the world through Pentecost but this one of which I am now going to speak, all the price that men paid would be as nothing. Listen! There has been more real divine research by the Holy Ghost into the nature of God and the nature of man in these last fifteen years than there ever was in any similar period in Christian history, and more intelligent discovery of God's action and working in and through man than ever before. That is God's divine laboratory of spiritual knowledge.

And when anyone comes to me with the statement that there is nothing in the baptism of the Holy Ghost but a psychological manifestation, I say, "Brother, sister, come with me and see the gems of God and the beautiful gold that has come out of the dross of dirty lives, and then you will know." Saved from sin and healed from disease—that is divine demonstration.

In my Assembly at Spokane is a real little woman who was blind for nine years. She had little teaching along the line of faith of God. She sat one day with her group of six children to discover that her dirty brute of a husband had abandoned her and his children and left her to starve. A debased human being is capable of things that no beast will do, for a beast will care for its own.

You can imagine what her little heart was like. She was crushed, broken, bruised, and bleeding. She gathered her children around her and began to pray. They were sitting on their front porch. Presently, one of them got up and said, "Oh, Mama, there is a man coming up the path and He looks like Jesus! And, oh, Mama, there is blood on His hands and blood on His feet!" And the children were frightened and ran around the corner of the house. After a while, the biggest one looked around the corner and said, "Why, Mama, He is laying His hands on your eyes!" And just then her blind eyes opened. That is divine power.

And, beloved, if we could have seen the reason, we would have seen that there were some Christians, like those at the Brooks' Home, Zion City, or some other place, who were praying the power of God on a hungry world, and Jesus Christ in His search for those who would receive, rushed to her and sent her forth to praise God and teach the gospel of Jesus.

I would not have missed my life in Africa for anything. It put me up against some of the real problems. I sat upon a mountain in Africa one afternoon and counted eleven hundred native villages within the range of my eyes. I could see the color of the grass on the mountains sixty miles away. I could see the mountains one hundred and fifty miles away, so clear was its rarefied atmosphere.

Then I began to figure, and I said, "Within the range of my eyes, there live ten million native people. They have never heard the name of Jesus. In the whole land, there are at least one hundred million people, perhaps two hundred million." They are being born at a tremendous rate. Do you know there are more heathen born every day than are Christianized in fifty years? When are we going to catch up by our present method of building schools and teaching them to read? Never! I tell you, it will never come that way. It has got to come from heaven by the power of God, by an outpouring of the Holy Ghost. That is divine salvation.

That is the reason my heart rejoices in the blessed promise, "In the last days, saith God, I will pour out of my Spirit upon all flesh" (Acts 2:17). And every last one of the two hundred million unsaved people is going to hear and know of the Lord Jesus Christ. Beloved, I would rather have a place in the kingdom of God, praying that thing into existence and praying the power of God upon them, than anything else in the world.

Africa is said to be the first settled country in the world, and we believe the world is six thousand years old. Africa has been settled for five thousand years. Two hundred or four hundred million have died every century. Split the difference and say that three hundred million have died every [century] for five thousand years.

It caused me to pray and meditate. I said, "Has God no interest in these people? And if He has an interest, why is not something done for them? What is the matter with God? Is God unable to help, or does He not care?" My heart was breaking under the burden of it. I said, "God, there must be an explanation somewhere. What is it, Lord? Tell me about it."

Then my heart grew calm, and the Spirit said, "The church, which is His body," and I knew that was God's answer.

I said, "Yes, the church should have sent missionaries and built schools and done this and that."

But the Spirit kept on saying, "The church, which is His body. The church, which is His body." I sat and listened to that voice repeat that sentence for a half hour.

I said, "My God, my soul begins to see. The church is the ministering presence of the Son of God in the world. The church is the generating agency of the power of God in the world. The church has been negligent in one great trust. She has not prayed the power of God out of heaven."

Then I saw what has become a conviction in my soul from that day: that there never was a soul born to God in the whole earth at any time until some soul in the world got hold of the living Spirit of God and generated that Spirit in saving grace and creative virtue and ministered it until it took possession of a soul, no difference if it was a million miles away. Thus, the life of Christ is begotten in them.

When I try to induce men to forget their little squabbles and little differences and go to praying, it is because my soul feels the burden of it. Mother Etter has been like a marshal for fifty years. The sick have been healed; people have been converted and blessed. But beloved, when I heard of Brother Brook's shutting himself up night and day to pray the power of God on a world, I said, "That is where she gets her fire; that is where it comes from to my soul; that is where it comes from to other souls—through those who pray." That is divine intercession.

Notice how beautifully this armory is lighted. The world lived in darkness for five thousand years, and they had no way of lighting a place like this except by torches or candles. But there was just as much electricity five thousand years ago as there is today. Somebody found how to handle it, discovered the laws that govern it, and learned to apply it to our need. But to this day, there is no man who can tell us what electricity is or what its substance is. We know we can control it this way and guide it that way and make it do this and that, but what it is nobody can tell us. However, down somewhere on the river there is a machine that is called a dynamo, and it draws the electricity out of the air and transmits it over the wires. And these days, they are sending it in wireless waves.

Do you know what prayer is? It is not begging God for this and that. The first thing we have to do is to get you beggars to quit begging, until a little faith moves in your soul. Prayer is God's divine generator. The spirit of man is God's divine dynamo. When you go to pray, your spirit gets into motion. Not ten thousand revolutions per minute, but possibly one hundred thousand. The voltage of heaven comes to your heart, and it flows from your hands, it burns into the souls of men, and God almighty's Spirit is applied through you to their need.

Over in Indiana some years ago was a farmer who used to be a friend of Brother Fockler and myself. His son had been in South America, had a dreadful case of typhoid fever and no proper nursing; the result was that he developed a great fever sore ten inches in diameter. The whole abdomen became grown up with proud flesh, one layer on top of another layer, until there were five layers. The nurse had to lift up those layers and wash it with an antiseptic to keep the maggots out of it.

When he exposed the body for me to pray for him, I was shocked. I never had seen anything like it before. As I went to pray for him, I spread my fingers out wide and put my hand right on that cursed growth of proud flesh. I prayed God in the name of Jesus Christ to blast the curse of hell and burn it up by the power of God. Then I took the train and came back to Chicago. The next day I received a telegram saying, "Lake, the most unusual thing has happened. An hour after you left, the whole print of your hand was burned into that growth a quarter of an inch deep."

You talk about the voltage of heaven and the power of God! Why, there is lightning in the soul of Jesus. The lightning of Jesus heals men by its flash; sin dissolves, disease flees when the power of God approaches.

And yet we are quibbling and wondering if Jesus Christ is big enough for our needs. Let's take the bars down. Let God come into your life. And in the name of Jesus your heart will not be satisfied with an empty Pentecost, but your soul will claim the light of God, and the lightning of Jesus will flood your life. Amen.

## CHAPTER 3

# DIVINE HEALING

---

IF THERE IS SOMETHING WRONG with a man's spirit, he goes directly to God, but the next day he has a pain in his back, and he goes down the road to the doctor's. Where do you get your right to do such a thing?

There is a wretched looseness about consecration to God. Christians do not seem to know what consecration to God means. What would you think of Jesus Christ, if you saw Him going down the road and into a doctor's office for some dope? Why, you would feel like apologizing for the Lord, wouldn't you? Well, He has just as much reason to apologize for you. When you became a Christian with a consecrated body, soul, and spirit, your privilege of running to the doctor was cut off forevermore.

"Faith cometh by hearing, and hearing by the word of God" (Romans 10:17). This young man who testified says he suffers because of an appetite for cigarettes, and he hopes that we will pray so that the next time he wants to smoke he won't. I tell you, God says, "Quit your sins and then come to Me, and I will pardon." He doesn't say, "You come on with your sins, and I will pardon you." He says, "You quit your meanness, you quit fooling with the doctor and the devil, you quit your secret habits and come to Me, and I will deliver you." That is the only road to God; that is the way in God.

So a Christian's consecration is not just a consecration of his spirit to God, not of his soul to God. It's a consecration of body and soul and spirit—the entire man, everything there is of us—and it cuts us forever plumb off from looking for help from the flesh, the world, or the devil.

There are three enemies of man: the world, the flesh, and the devil. Our nature has three departments: spirit and soul and body. What would you think of the Christian who would go to the devil or to some deceitful spirit to find balm for his spirit? Why, you would think he was not a Christian at all, nor would he be. Suppose a man wants peace for his soul (mind), and he appeals to the spirit of the world or the flesh to get it. You would not think he was a Christian at all. Then how will you consider a man who wants healing for his body and goes to the world and man to get it?

I am going to preach to you for five minutes out of the fifth [chapter] of James. He is very explicit in this matter. He is not laying down rules for the people of the world. He is talking straight to the Christians. "Is any among you [Christians] afflicted? let him pray" (James 5:13), not "let him go to the devil or the doctor or some human source."

"Is any sick among you? Let him call for the elders of the church" (verse 14) means this: if you have prayed and deliverance has not come, unquestionably it is a weakness of your faith. You need help. Then the next thing is, "Let him call for the elders of the church; and let them pray over him, anointing him with oil in the name of the Lord"

(James 5:14).

When I was preaching in Washington, D.C., recently, an old sister said she had anointed her little girl the night before and she had put a whole bottle full of oil all over her. So you see, she was not looking to God to heal; she expected the anointing oil to heal. Satan is a subtle old devil, but the Lord gives us fight. He says not the anointing of oil, but "the prayer of faith shall save the sick, and the Lord shall raise him up" (verse 15). That is why I never use oil except when requested to do so, because people are looking to the anointing oil instead of to the Lord God. "Let him call for the elders of the church; and let them pray over him, anointing him with oil in the name of the Lord: and the prayer of faith shall save the sick," not the anointing oil. The use of anointing oil is a matter of obedience. It is a symbol of the Spirit of God, and that is all it is. So we place upon the individual the anointing oil in order that we fulfill the symbol of the Spirit of God as the Healer, and that is all.

"The prayer of faith shall save the sick, and the Lord shall raise him up; and if he have committed sins, they shall be forgiven him" (verse 15). Thus, he goes on and makes the teaching broader.

One of the beautiful things about the gospel of Jesus Christ is that it is progressive in its revelation and application. First, we were asked to pray if we are afflicted. Second, we were asked to call for the elders. Then, the Lord goes down to the real business in a man's heart. "Confess your faults one to another" (James 5:16). Get your old tattling, blatting tongue tied up, and confess to the other party that you have been tattling.

If all the Christians had that gag in their mouths, there would not be half as much shouting in the meetings as there is. Now listen, I don't want to pound people on the head, but I want to teach you a lesson. Here is the broad principle of the gospel: "Confess your faults."

When I went to Africa, I had the advantage of getting

on absolutely new ground that no one had spoiled with a lot of loose teaching. In this country, our people have been slobbered over with teaching that doesn't amount to anything, and they wobble this way and that way, "like a wave of the sea driven with the wind and tossed." And God says, "Let not that man think that he shall receive any thing of the Lord" (James 1:6–7).

One day, as a young man, God brought me in to see my own need when I needed healing from heaven. There was nobody to pray for me, and I was not even a Christian in the best sense of being a Christian. I was a member of a Methodist church, but I had seen God heal one dear soul, who was very dear to me. As I sat alone one day, I said, "Lord, I am finished with the doctor and with the devil. I am finished with the world and the flesh, and from today I lean on the arm of God." I committed myself to God; and God almighty, right there and then, though there was no sign of healing or anything else, accepted my consecration to Him. That disease that had stuck on my life and almost killed me for nearly nine years was gone. It was chronic constipation. I would take three ounces of castor oil at a single dose, three times a week.

The place of strength and the place of victory is the place of consecration to God. It is when a man shuts his teeth and says, "I go with God this way," that victory is going to come.

My! This wobbling business makes one think of the old Irish woman who was on a ship in a storm. When the ship rolled one way, she would say, "O good Lord," and when the ship would plunge to the other side, she would say, "Good devil." When someone asked her why she did that, she said, "Why, how can I tell into whose arms I will fall?"

May the Lord wake us up in our souls and get us out of this wobbly state and get us where we all commit ourselves once and for all and forever to almighty God, and then live by it and die by it.

People say, like the dear soul last night who sent word

to the meeting, "I am very sick, and if I don't get deliverance, I will have to do something." Why, sure you can do something—you can die. You ought to die instead of insulting and denying the Lord Jesus Christ and turning your back on Him. People say, "I can't die." Yes, you can, if you are not a coward, but you cannot sin. And it is just as much a sin to commit your body to the Lord Jesus Christ and then to turn to the doctor as it is to go and commit adultery or any other sin. It is a violation of your consecration to God.

Make a consecration to God and stand by that and live by that and be willing to die by that. Then you will grow up into God, where your faith is active enough to get answers to prayer.

There is no man who lives and has the ministry of healing that could pray for all the sick people. There are so many of them. Why, you come to an assembly like this, and every old saint who has a stomachache will come and ask you to pray for them, and there is no time for anything else. God wants us to grow up into Him where we get answers to prayer for ourselves. Then, if there is an extreme case and your faith is broken, confess your faults one to another and get the rest of the people to pray for you; and then in the extreme cases, send for the elders of the church—that is the mind of God.

In the twelfth chapter of 1 Corinthians, the nine gifts of the Holy Spirit are enumerated.

For to one is given by the Spirit the word of wisdom; to another the word of knowledge by the same Spirit; to another faith by the same Spirit; to another the gifts of healing by the same Spirit; to another the working of miracles; to another prophecy; to another discerning of spirits; to another divers kinds of tongues; to another the interpretation of tongues. (1 Corinthians 12:8–10)

These are the gifts or enablements that are given by God to certain [ones] in the church. Now, here is a thought I want to leave with you. We go over into

Ephesians, and we see a different order: not the gifts of enablements are mentioned, but the gifts in this case are individuals. It is men to whom God has given definite ministries.

And in the church of Jesus Christ not only should the gifts exist, but also the faith to use them. And they do exist if they are developed, and they are workable when the faith in your heart is made active to use them. But you can have the gifts right out of heaven, and if the faith in your heart is not active, you cannot operate them.

There is only one prayer that is answered. It is not prayer that is answered but the prayer of faith. It is the prayer of faith that shall save the sick. Believing prayer is not much noise. Believing prayer may not be any noise at all. Believing prayer is a committing, an intelligent committing of yourself to God; and your mind is stayed in God and your heart is stayed in God and you are walking in God. You are ready to die rather than go to anyone but God. That is the real believing prayer. That is the continuous prayer. That is prevailing prayer. Blessed be God!

So in Ephesians, the Word of God tells us that there are some apostles, some prophets, some teachers, some evangelists, and some pastors. (See Ephesians 4:11.) These are God's gifts, these men—not gifts as they are mentioned in Corinthians, but men are mentioned in Ephesians—and the men with ministries are God's gift to the church until such time as they shall all come, the entire body of Christ, into the unity of the faith, into the likeness of Jesus Christ, into the measure of the stature of the Son of God. "Till we all come" (Ephesians 4:12), not one or two. Blessed be His precious name!

These things will demonstrate to you how far we are behind the gospel ideal. We are so far behind. A few years ago, many commonly believed that when the baptism of the Holy Ghost was being poured out upon the world, that we were the particular little lot who were to be the bride of

Christ and go with Him when He came. But pretty soon it began to dawn on those who looked into the Word that there was not even a tangible body of Christ yet. The body of Christ is the members called of God, united in one spirit and in one hope of their calling—blessed be God—with one Lord, one faith, and one baptism. That is the body. Then all the other developments, the bride, and all the rest of it are born out of the body. (See Ephesians 4:2–6.)

God is getting a body at this present time, and in the body of Christ, the orderly body of Christ, the unified body, He wants to bring it forth today. He has set His gifts: the word of wisdom, knowledge, faith, gifts of healing, etc. He has set likewise men: apostles, prophets, evangelists, pastors, and teachers.

> For the perfecting of the saints, for the work of the ministry, for the edifying of the body of Christ: till we all come in the unity of the faith, and of the knowledge of the Son of God, unto a perfect man, unto the measure of the statute of the fullness of Christ. (Ephesians 4:12–13)

Now healing is not a difficult matter. It does not take a bit more faith to be healed from your sickness than it does to be saved from your sins. The only difference is that in your own consciousness, you knew there was no place to get forgiveness except from God. You had sense enough to know you could not get it from the devil; you had to get it from the Lord.

But your body gets sick and your consciousness, because of your education, permits you to go to the doctor or the sorcerers or the devil, and the one is just as offensive to God as the other. The Christian body and soul and spirit are one [unit]. A real Christian has committed his whole being unto the living God; he has consecrated himself to Jesus Christ with all the fullness that Jesus consecrated Himself to the Father at the river Jordan. He was baptized. He consecrated Himself unto the uttermost, unto "all righteousness" (Matthew 3:15), unto everything that was right, unto the will of God forever. Blessed be His name.

Now there are examples in the Word of God that are very striking along this line. You listen to the Word of God: "Cursed be the man that trusteth in man" (Jeremiah 17:5). Talk about your running to the doctor. That is what the Lord thinks about it. "Cursed be the man that trusteth in man, and maketh flesh his arm, and whose heart departeth from the Lord." And the Word of God in the fourteenth [chapter] of 2 Chronicles gives us a most remarkable example of Asa, the king of Israel, who trusted God when the great armies of their enemies came up against them. He went down on his knees before God, and he said,

> Lord, it is nothing with thee to help, whether with many, or with them that have no power: help us, O Lord our God; for we rest on thee, and in thy name we go against this multitude O Lord, thou art our God; let no man prevail against thee. (2 Chronicles 14:11)

Their little handful of men conquered the whole mob.

But after a while, Asa got a disease in his feet, and the Word says his disease became exceeding great; and in his disease he trusted not the Lord, but the physicians; and Asa died. It is recorded against him as an offense against God that he failed to trust God for the disease in his feet, but instead trusted the physicians. (See 2 Chronicles 16:12–13.)

Somebody says, "Well, all right, I will commit myself to the Lord, and then of course, I will not have any more stomachache. I will just be kept, etc." Maybe you will if your faith in God stands strong enough, and perhaps you won't if it does not. But there is one thing that stands—that is, your consecration to God. If your faith fails, it does not make any difference; you stand consecrated to God just the same. If you do not get an answer to prayer, you are consecrated to God just the same; and if God almighty has got to let the devil thrash you half to death for a week or two months or longer, you take it until the [fault] that the Lord is after is out of your life and faith has conquered. Then you will learn obedience to God by the things you suffer (see Hebrews 5:8.) That is the only way.

People go around cursing the devil all the time. [When] you go in the ways of the devil, you get crooked in your soul and proud in your heart, and that cuts you off from God, and you are left in the hands of the devil. The wisest thing to do with you is just like I did with one of my sons. I said, "Young man, you just take your own way until you bump your head against the wall." When he was hurt almost to death, he was glad to come back to his old dad to be helped out.

We know the Word of God so well, so in our proud hearts we say, "We have been baptized in the Holy Ghost," and all that kind of attitude. It is just as offensive to God as it can be, and God has just got to draw back His hand and let you go, like I did my son. And then you will come down with some old disease, and you will lay and fret and fume and cry until you get right with God and open your heart to God; then He will rebuke the devourer, and He will take the thing away. Bless God.

I used to be a member of a church where it was considered just as offensive to take medicine or go to the doctor as it was to go to the devil for health. The Christian who would run to a doctor was on a level with the adulterer or the thief. That is absolutely right. That is according to the Word of God. A whole consecration of your whole being—your body and soul and spirit—is what Jesus demands. It is what Jesus asks and, bless God, that is the only place that is worthwhile.

We go around talking and shouting about the almighty Christ and what He can do and what He is, etc. But the first time we get a stomachache, away we go to the doctor and get a dose, and the almighty Christ gets a slap in the face.

Beloved, you listen to me. If there are any people in all the world who ought to be taught of God, who ought to be walking with God, who ought to be consecrated to all the will of God, it is the Christian people, especially those who are baptized in the Holy Ghost. It ought to be absolutely unnecessary for any man at this day to even speak of these things in a public service. We ought to have been so committed from the first day to the Lord Jesus Christ that the committing of ourselves to any man for anything would be highly offensive to our spirits. And if we saw our brother or sister becoming weak and falling into the hands of man, our prayer and love and faith and sympathy ought to get under them as though they were falling into the habit of drinking whiskey again.

It is just as offensive for the Christian to take medicine as for the drunkard to take whiskey. Don't you see, beloved, the great wonderful advantage in the Christian's life of becoming cut clear and free from all dependence on the arm of man? You are cut forever from the world, from the flesh, from the devil. Bless God.

I had a friend in Africa who was greatly distressed because he could not learn to swim. Finally, one day he got drunk and walked off the docks into the sea at Cape Town into about five hundred feet of water, and he could swim after that, all right.

Don't you see, beloved, that you will never have faith in God in the world until you launch out into God, until you commit yourself to God and then either live or die? I belong to God; I am done with man, and I am done with leaning on his arm.

I know what these things are. In my home I had seven children. They were born without medicine. One dear brother testified the other night that the Lord had kept disease out of the home. It was not that way in mine. There wasn't a devilish thing that came down the road that my family did not get, from pneumonia, smallpox, and typhoid fever to a shooting accident, and God let us be tested right up and down the line.

It is one thing to get down on your knees and say, "I commit my body, my soul, my spirit to God," and it is another thing to stand by your baby until you hear it gasp, and it is another thing to close its eyes in death if necessary, but I am not going back on my Lord. That is the kind of training I got, and that is the clearness in faith my heart cries out for.

Maybe in another generation we will have a multitude of people who stand in God like giants, and we can have a manifestation of the sons of God and take the world for God and crown the Christ King of Kings and Lord of Lords.

Now, I do not preach to anybody else what I have not been through myself. I tell you, the Lord has let me go through the mill. One time I got inflammatory rheumatism, and for nine months I suffered. I guess I did. But I shut my teeth and I said, "You devil, you can't put me in bed; I won't go," and I dragged myself home, and I would get in bed and feel like crying out in my agony. At the end of nine months, God had wrought one thing in my heart: that if I died, the devil would not get me to take medicine again. One day I felt in my spirit I needed help. There was nobody there that could pray for me. So I got on a train and went to Chicago to John Alexander Dowie. One day there was a company of people like this, and when I came along, it was so packed full I could not even look into the door. After a while, there were some other people who couldn't get in. Finally an old man, an elder, came along and prayed for us out there; and as he did, I was healed from the crown of my head to the soles of my feet. Years after, he told me that was the only healing he ever had that he knew about.

I often wondered if the virtue came through the old brother or not, but God met my faith. Do you not see, to commit yourself to God means something? I tell you, it is probably going to mean some suffering someday, but that is the way of clearness, the way of truth. That is the way you can look every man in the face and say, "I am not leaning on the arm of flesh; I am going God's way."

We are such a weak, wobbly lot in these latter days. God is just trying to get some backbone in us. We come along and are baptized, and about a week after, we can find them doing all sorts of things. The Christians in the old days came down to be baptized, and as they did so, a Roman officer took their names and sent them up to Rome. Instantly their citizenship was canceled, their right of protection from Roman government was cut off, their goods were confiscated, and they were left as prey to the avarice of the people, but they got baptized just the same. Bless God.

I tell you, that is the kind of people that thirty million of them gave their lives to God in the first four centuries and were blotted out of the world in various ways. Thirty million of them! There was some Christian spirit, and there was some consecration to God in those days. It was poverty or death or sickness or prison or anything else, but it was God's way of consecration. I tell you, God will meet that kind of thing. If they lived, all right, and if they died, all right. They belonged to God, and the world ever since, for 1400 years, looks back with pride to that list of people who gave themselves to the Lord God. They put the stamp of character on the Christian world. Bless God.

All the heroes, bless God, did not live back there either. You come down to the history of Scotland, to the Covenanters. They wrote a covenant and said, "We will have nae King but Jesus," and you can see the old Scottish man shut his teeth and, opening a vein in his arm, sign the covenant with his own blood. And three hundred thousand of them gave their lives then to make that covenant good and died saying, "We will have nae King but Jesus."

Now you listen to me. I will guarantee to you that if there are fifty sick people in this room, and you commit yourselves to God in that spirit and with that reality, bless God, you won't need anybody to pray for you. You will just get well. Bless God. The devil cannot come around you when that kind of thing is in your soul.

One of my sons was dying with pneumonia once. I prayed for that fellow, and I prayed for him, and it was not a bit of good. But one day I was downtown, and I was praying about that boy, and the Lord said, "You go home and confess your sins to your wife."

And I said, "I will." I stopped and got one of the old elders to come down to my house. As we rode along, we talked together, and I said, "I have some things I want to fix up with my wife before you pray. There have been all kinds of prayer, but He won't hear." So I took my wife in the other room and told her the whole business, all there was; and we went into the other room and prayed for that son, and he was healed in a second.

I want to tell you that when Christians are not healed, as a rule, you get digging around and get the Holy Ghost to help you; and when they have vomited out all the stuff, they will get the healing.

You listen to me. Healing comes straight down from God. All man is, is a medium through which God can work. God is a Spirit; He needs embodiment. He chooses man as a body. The church is the body. "Know ye not that ye are the temple of God, and that the Spirit of God dwelleth in you?" (1 Corinthians 3:16). There is something that gets into your spirit or into your body that is obstructing the free flow of the Spirit of God. Get that thing out; it is between you and God.

I tell you, when you line people up so they will trust God for their bodies as they do for their souls, there will not be one half the backsliding there is now. I was a member of a body of one hundred thousand people, and I never heard of such a thing as any of them backsliding. They stood for God, and they died for God. The character was in them, and they did not know half as much about God as we do by the revelation of the Spirit in these days.

I am twice as anxious this afternoon about this great body of people here, to know whether or not they are going to commit themselves clear in God, than I am about the sick. There may be dozens in this room who are so very sick that they need God. But, beloved, listen. Suppose one of them was not healed and the rest were made clear in their consecration to God; you would have a bigger demonstration.

As fast as you get them healed, the Christians without Christ's consecration are down in their faith and becoming sick. After a while, a preacher gets to be a kind of doctor of saints in his little assembly. God does not want it. Get clear; get straight in your consecration to God. Put yourself body and soul and spirit forever in God's hands. Do it today, bless God. Do it today.

How ashamed a Christian ought to be that he is trusting in the arm of flesh or in a medicine bottle somewhere around the house! You go home and gather up the abominable stuff and put it in the alley box [a garbage pail] and then apologize to the alley box.

You cannot tell me anything about medicine. There never was a bigger humbug practiced on mankind than the practice of medicine. The biggest men in the medical world have declared it over and over again, but the mob does not pay any attention to it.

Professor Douglas McLaggen, who had the chair of medical jurisprudence, stood up among one thousand students, when asked to lecture on the science of medicine, and he said, "I am an honest man, and 'An honest man is the noblest work of God'; from the days of Hippocrates and Galen until now, we have been stumbling in the dark, from diagnosis to [illegible]." Sir Ashley Cooper, who was physician to Queen Victoria for twenty-five years, the greatest physician in Great Britain, said, "The science of medicine is founded upon conjecture and improved by murder." Dr. Magendie of Paris, who has the greatest system of diagnosis in the world, said, "We take up the attention of the patient with our medicine, while nature cuts in and makes a cure." But you cannot tell a third-rate American doctor that.

Yet, the Christian world turns its back on the Son of God and goes and puts itself in the hands of men. No man who ever lived, or ever will live, will ever reduce the subject of medicine to a science. No two doses of medicine will ever produce the same effect in your own person. You can take a dose of medicine today and another tomorrow, and you will have a different effect tomorrow than you had today.

That may be all right for the world. Why, the man who is not a Christian has got to have a physician of some kind, but the Christian can't. God cut the privilege off long ago. Bless God. "Is any sick among you [Christians]? Let him call for the elders of the church" (James 5:14). That is all the privilege the Word of God gives him. That is the way in to God, on the line of divine healing. Bless God.

Bless God, I tell you, I am just looking for the day when there will be a great, blessed, true company of men and women in this world who will stand in this through the living God just as clear as crystal, who have cut clear off from the world, the flesh, and the devil. That is the characteristic of the church of Philadelphia all right.

God has let me see healings in every way that human eyes can see them. I have seen them come like the flash of lightning. I have seen the Spirit of God flash around the room, just like the lightning. God was there in lightning form, and the devils were cast out and the sick healed. I have seen God come as the tender bud when nobody knew He was there, and people were healed. I have seen people healed in the audiences when cancers would melt away and varicose veins were healed. Nobody prayed for them. They just put themselves in the hands of God. That is all.

There is no man who lives who can define the operations of faith in a man's heart. But there is one thing we are sure of: that when we cut ourselves off from every other help, we never find the Lord Jesus Christ to fail. If there is any failure, it is our failure, not God's. Bless God.

CHAPTER 4

# THE GRACE OF DIVINE HEALING

I WANT TO USE A FAMILIAR TEXT, "The grace of God that bringeth salvation hath appeared to all men." Titus 2:11. There never was a bigger word than the word of "Grace." If we undertake to define and analyze its operations, that beautiful term brings the many-sided gospel of Jesus Christ to the heart with a wonderful clearness. The Grace of Jesus Christ is not His demeanor, neither His beautiful gratuitous giving. It is the DIVINE OUTFLOWING OF THE NATURE OF GOD, heavenly, healing loveliness, and holy balm, it comes to the needy world; not only as a sin-saving action of God, but as a healing virtue, pains, changing the very chemicalization of their being, healing and abiding rest in God. Divine healing is no mystery. It is the definite action of the Spirit of God in the souls and the bodies of men.

There is a Grace of God that rests on a community. There is a Grace of God that rests upon a church; the Grace of God that rests upon an individual. In South Africa, there used to be an old lady who visited our home once in a while. She was one of the sweetest, most blessed creatures I ever met. My, when she came into my office and sat down for five minutes, she brought the consciousness of God, a restfulness and a peace of mind. From her whole person there seemed to radiate that blessedness that can be described only as the grace of God, and the very atmosphere would become pregnant with it. I would make excuses to take her through the house. I wanted her to leave that beautiful communion all over the place. Because when she was gone, it seemed the house settled down, the noisy children ceased to influence, and all invisible unrest disappeared. It was the Grace of God.

Tuesday of this week, at Portland, we had an experience with a young woman who was on the way to the river to take her life. Somehow she felt impelled to come up to our healing rooms. She sat for a little while and we talked to her, soothed her heart, and tried to get her to God. I said to those present, "I wish someone could take her and love her for a little while." Soon a lady of our church came in and I introduced her to the poor girl. I said, "Just take her home with you. Put your arms around her and let her feel your love. Let her know what the Grace of God is, not by preaching, but by contact." She took her home and four days later the young woman came back, after having given her heart to God. In the meantime things worked out in her family; she went back home to be a blessing to her brother, her sister and dear old parents and the kingdom of God. This is the same Grace of healing that flowed from the loving Hands and heavenly Spirit of Jesus.

I wonder when the Lord Jesus Christ passed down the

highway as He walked from Bethany to Jerusalem, if the atmosphere was not alive, pregnant with the beautiful light of His Divine presence and blessing. And I haven't a bit of doubt that when someone walked down that way after Jesus passed, and they breathed the air that Jesus breathed, that they felt the life of God that was shed from His person, and were healed by the virtue of the fact that Christ had been there. That same healing Grace permeated the atmosphere around dear old Peter, so that the sick were healed as far from him as his eventide shadow reached.

That is my ideal of a Christian heart, a Christian life, a Christian church or a Christian ministry.

My soul desires, by the Grace of God, that out through these old brick walls, there will flow that beautiful emanation of Christ throughout old Chicago, that will discover disease in every part of the city, and heal both soul and body. That this Grace may bring to the heart of man made free from sin's power, a life joined to God, a consciousness of holy oneness with our Father God, through Jesus Christ. Atonement makes at-one-ment, in body, souls and spirit with Christ, both in salvation through Him and in ministry for Him.

How blessed it is when once in a while we walk suddenly into the presence of one rich with the light and life of God. As we emerge from the storms of life, as we come out of the turmoil, passing into the presence of the heart that balm and sweetness indicating the presence of God, and leaving upon our life a divine influence that gives us restfulness of mind, restfulness of heart, and sunlit soul, the God-lit life, instantly there comes to the quiet in God.

There is the Grace of God that goes underneath the soul of man, that by the blessed gift of the Spirit, lifts from the life forever the shadows and darkness that sin has brought, and takes away the corrosion that has come upon the soul of man, and by the Grace of God lets the heart of man understand the blessed touch of the Son of God that imparts eternal life. Blessed be His name.

> "Down in the human heart, crushed by the tempter,
> Feelings lie buried that Grace can restore.
> Touched by a loving heart, wakened by kindness,
> Chords that were broken will vibrate once more."

O yes beloved, there is a Grace of God that goes underneath the life and lifts the nature of man into beautiful holiness and heavenly contact, into the consciousness of purity, the realization of power, blessed be His name forever.

One morning a distress call came from a woman on behalf of her husband. Some other ministers and I responded. We found the man in delirium tremens, begging his wife for just a little more whiskey, and making the usual promises an insane man will make. We knelt by his bed, laid hand upon him, lifted our hearts in love and faith to God. "The grace that bringeth salvation" appeared, stole into that man's soul, and in five minutes his pains were gone, the curse had departed, and he never wanted whiskey again. Later he called on me in Portland, Oregon, took my hands and poured out his tears and love for God, told of his success in life, and all the rest of the beautiful story. The Lord was not in the cyclone, or in the fire, or in the earthquake. He is now as then in the still small voice and the healing touch of Divine gentleness.

Every soul should have its own contact with God. If that touch has not been real to your own heart yet, it may become real. Bless God!

Mrs. Graham was dying of pneumonia. As I entered into her home I was met by Brother Fogwill, coming out. He said, "John, you are too late. She is gone." The flames of God came over my heart and though she had not breathed for twenty-three minutes, the breath and the power of Christ came upon her and she is continuing her ministry for God and man.

## DIVINE HEALING: A GIFT FROM GOD

Beloved, the Christian life is a glorious doorway into God, through Jesus Christ, into the divinest secrets that the soul of man ever desired to attain. And bless His Name, you and I tonight are privileged to enter that doorway, and to know Him "whom to know is life eternal."

Some days past, Dr. McInturff and I were called to the bedside of a woman that was dying. She had gone out of her mind. Had become unconscious, and was then in the coma of death. Her nurse told us that she had not been able to speak, hear, or see for a number of days. We knelt, prayed, and left, with a feeling that God was there, though we could detect no action in the woman's body so far as we could tell. We went away with the consciousness that our prayer was heard, and the work was done.

Weeks passed and there was no report of the woman's condition. Until finally one day the mother-in-law of the woman walked into the office to tell how wonderfully God had healed and delivered the woman. Later the lady herself, walked in, and for an half hour told of the wonderful inner action of the Spirit that went into her life even as we prayed. She said, "Brother, as you knelt by my bedside, I became conscious that someone was there. All I knew was that the sound of the voices was different from others. Then you proceeded to put your hands on my head, and something began to steal down through my brain; the awful torture gradually subsided. After awhile I became still and quiet in my soul. Then a voice began to speak to me about my Lord and Saviour Jesus Christ. It bade me have faith in God, and said that I should come out of this condition, and be a blessing to my home and husband. I have now come to tell you that your prayer was heard." We never spoke of the Grace of salvation, but the living presence of the Spirit came to her and made her to know of "the grace of God that bringeth salvation."

The world is in need of a knowledge of Christ's way of salvation and healing. The whole subject of its actuality has become greatly dimmed in the hearts of men. There is a dire need of a wondrous clarifying of the spiritual atmosphere, in order that His power may be made effective to those who turn their hearts thither-ward. This then is a part of the mission of Pentecost. Not only to declare Christ as a Savior and a Healer, but to manifest Him by God's Grace in daily life, through God-anointed lives and hands to carry that blessed Grace of God, and transmit it to whosoever will. Put your hands on the sick, believer; Jesus Christ commanded it, and "they shall recover." I am praying that upon your souls there will come the presence of God, through Christ, that will make you realize yourself as a minister of the Lord and Savior, with a mission from God, and that in His Name you too, my brother and sister, will go forth to carry this light and power to whosoever will.

A young man dying of consumption came to our healing rooms and said, "I am no Christian. I have not been interested in religion. I have heard that people are healed here. I am dying and have no hope. Tell me what you have to say in the shortest words you can." I answered, "Young man, God is able to deliver you. He is able to heal you. He is ready to do it right now." He replied, "I haven't any faith." I said, "But I am a child of God, I am a son of God, and I have faith." And without more ado I proceeded to pray. That man was healed. His sister was converted and healed, and other members of the family were saved. I received word telling of a movement of God in the community, where a dozen people are now seeking God unto salvation.

## CHAPTER 5

# BEHOLD, I GIVE YOU POWER

---

MATTHEW 8:1-2: "When He was come down from the mountain, great multitudes followed Him, and behold, there came a leper and worshipped Him, saying, 'Lord, if thou wilt, thou canst make me clean.'"

That man knew that Jesus had the power to heal him, but he did not know it was God's will, and that Jesus had committed Himself to the healing of mankind. If he had known he would have said, "Lord, heal me."

It is always God's will to heal. Our faith may fail. My faith failed to the extent that unless someone else had gone under my life and prayed for me, I would have died. But God was just as willing to heal me as He could be. It was my faith that broke down. God is willing, just as willing to heal as He is to save. Healing is a part of salvation. It is not separate from salvation. Healing was purchased by the blood of Jesus. This book always connects salvation and healing.

David said: "Bless the Lord, O my soul, and forget not all His benefits: Who forgiveth all thine iniquities; Who healeth all thy diseases" (Psalm 103:2,3).

There never has been a man in the world who was converted, and was sick at the same time, who might not have been healed if he had believed God for it. But he was not instructed in faith to believe God for healing.

Suppose two men came to the altar. One is sick and lame; the other is a sinner. Suppose they knelt at the altar together. The sinner says, "I want to find the Lord." Everyone in the house will immediately lend the love of their heart and the faith of their soul to help him touch God. But the lame fellow says, "I have a lame leg or my spine is injured. I want healing." Instead of everybody lending their love and faith in the same way to that man, everybody puts up a question mark.

That comes because of the fact we are instructed on the Word of God concerning the salvation of the soul, but our education concerning sickness and His desire and willingness to heal had been neglected. We have gone to the eighth or the tenth grade or the university on the subject of salvation, but on the subject of healing we are in the A,B,C class.

Verse 3. "Jesus put forth His hand, and touched him, saying, 'I will be thou clean.'" Did He ever say anything in the world but "I will", or did He ever say, "I cannot heal you because it is not the will of God", or "I cannot heal you because you are being purified by this sickness", or "I cannot heal you because you are glorifying God in this sickness"? There is no such instance in the book.

On the other hand we are told "He healed ALL that came to Him." Never a soul ever applied to God for salvation or healing that Jesus did not save and heal! Did you ever think what calamity it might have been if a man had come to Jesus once and said, "Lord, save me", and the Lord had said, "No, I cannot save you". Every man forevermore would have a question mark as to whether or not God would save him. There would not be a universal confidence as there is today.

Suppose Jesus had ever said to a sick man, "No, I cannot heal you". You would have the same doubt about healing. The world would have settled back and said, "Well, it may be God's will to heal that man or that woman, but I do not know whether or not it is His will to heal me."

Jesus Christ did not leave us in doubt about God's will, but when the Church lost her faith in God, she began to teach the people that maybe it was not God's will to heal them. So the Church introduced the Phrase, "If it be Thy will" concerning healing. But Jesus "healed all that came to Him" (Matt. 4:23; Luke 9:6; Luke 9:11).

Notice what it says in Isaiah 35, "He will come and save you. Then the eyes of the blind shall be opened, and the ears of the deaf shall be unstopped. Then shall the lame man leap as an hart, and the tongue of the dumb shall sing." Salvation and healing connected!

Matthew 8:17. "That it might be fulfilled which was spoken by Isaiah the prophet, saying, Himself took our infirmities and BARE OUR SICKNESSES." And lest we might be unmindful of that great fact that he "bare our sicknesses and carried our sorrows", Peter emphasises it by saying, "Who his own self bare our sins in His own body on the tree, that we being dead to sins, should live unto righteousness: by whose stripes ye were healed" (1 Peter 2:24). Not "by whose stripes ye are healed", but "by whose stripes ye were healed". The only thing that is necessary is to believe, God. God's mind never needs to act for a man's salvation. He gave the Lord and Saviour Jesus Christ to die for you. God cannot go any farther in expressing His will in His desire to save man. The only thing that is necessary is to believe God. There is salvation by blood. There is salvation by power that actually comes of God into a man's life. The blood provided the power. Without the blood there would have been no power. Without the sacrifice there would have never been any glory. Salvation by blood, salvation by power.

The Church in general is very clear in her faith on the subject of salvation through the sacrifice of the Lord and Saviour Jesus Christ. The Christian world in general, regardless of their personal state of salvation, has a general faith and belief of the Lord and Saviour Jesus Christ for the salvation of the world. But they are ever in doubt and very inexperienced on the power of God.

Matthew 8:1-4. "When He was come down from the mountain, great multitudes followed Him. And, behold, there came a leper and worshipped Him, saying, 'Lord, if thou wilt, thou canst make me clean.' And Jesus put forth His hand, and touched him, saying, 'I will, be thou clean.' And immediately his leprosy was cleansed. And Jesus saith unto him, 'See thou tell no man; but go thy way, shew thyself to the priest, and offer the gift that Moses commanded, for a testimony unto them.'"

Did you ever stop to think that they have no medical remedy for the real things that kill folks? Typhoid fever: Fill the patient with a tankful of medicine and he will go right on for twenty-one days.

In 1913, I was in Chicago in a big meeting when I received a telegram from the hospital in Detroit, saying, "Your son, Otto, is sick with typhoid fever. If you want to see him, come." I rushed for a train, and when I arrived I found him in a ward. I told the man in charge I would like a private room for him so I could get a chance to pray for him. Well, God smote that thing in five minutes. I stayed with him for a couple of days until he was up and walking around. He went along for four or five weeks, and one day, to my surprise, I got another telegram telling me he had a relapse of typhoid. So I went back again. This time there was no sunburst of God like the first time.

Everything was as cold as steel, and my, I was so conscious of the power of the devil. I could not pray audibly, but I sat down by his bed and shut my teeth, and I said in my soul, "Now, Mr. Devil, go to it. You kill him if you can." And I sat there five days and nights. He did not get healing the second time instantly. It was healing by process because of the fact my soul took hold on God. I sat with my teeth shut, and I never left his bedside until it was done.

You may be healed like a sunburst of God today, and tomorrow. The next week or the next month when you want healing you may have to take it on the slow process. The action of God is not always the same because the conditions are not always the same.

In the life of Jesus people were instantly healed. I believe Jesus has such a supreme measure of the Spirit that when He put His hands on a man he was filled and submerged in the Holy Ghost, and the diseases withered-out and vanished.

But, beloved, you and I use the measure of the Spirit that we possess. (You can, as a member of His body, possess the Spirit in the same measure as He. God does not expect us to fulfil John 14:12 with less equipment than Jesus had. W. H. Reidt) And if we haven't got as much of God as Jesus had, then you pray for a man today, and you get a certain measure of healing, but he is not entirely well. The only thing to do is to pray for him tomorrow, and let him get some more, and keep on until he is well.

That is where people blunder. They will pray for a day or two, and then they quit. You pray and keep on day by day and minister to your sick until they are well. One of the things that has discredited healing is that evangelists will hold meetings, and hundreds of sick will come and be prayed for. In a great meeting like that you get a chance to pray once and do not see them again. You pray for ten people, and as a rule you will find that one or two or three are absolutely healed, but the others are only half healed, or quarter healed or have only a little touch of healing. It is just the same with salvation. You bring ten to the altar. One is saved and is clear in his soul. Another may come for a week, and another for a month before he is clear in his soul. The difference is not with God. The difference is inside the man. His consciousness has not opened up to God.

Every law of the Spirit that applies to salvation applies to healing likewise.

"And when Jesus was entered into Capernaum, there came unto Him a centurion, beseeching Him, and saying, 'Lord, my servant lieth at home sick of the palsy, grievously tormented.' And Jesus saith unto him, 'I will come and heal him.' The centurion answered and said, 'Lord, I am not worthy that thou shouldst come under my roof, but speak the word only, and my servant shall be healed.'" (Matthew 8:5-8). Here is healing at a distance. That centurion understood divine authority, and the same divine authority is vested in the Christian, for Jesus is the pattern for a Christian.

"For I am a man under authority, having soldiers under me: and I say to this man, Go, and he goeth; and to another, Come, and he cometh and to my servant, Do this, and he doeth it" (Verse 9).

The same divine authority that was vested in Jesus is vested by Jesus in every Christian soul. Jesus made provision for the Church of Jesus Christ to go on forever and do the same as He did, and to keep on doing them forever. That is what is the matter with the Church. The Church has lost faith in that truth. The result, they went on believing He could save them from sin, but the other great range of Christian life was left to the doctors and the devil or anything else. And the Church will never be a real Church, in the real power of the living God again, until she comes back again to the original standard where Jesus was.

Jesus said, "Behold, I give you authority." What authority? "Over unclean spirits to cast them out, and to heal all manner of sickness and all manner of disease" (Matthew 10:1). Jesus has vested that authority in you. You say, "Well, Lord, we understand the authority that is in your Word, but we haven't the power." But Jesus said, "Ye shall receive power, after that the Holy Ghost is come upon you" (Acts 1:8).

Now the Holy Ghost is come upon every Christian in a measure. It is a question of degree. There are degrees of the measure of the Spirit of God in men's lives. The baptism of the Holy Spirit is a greater measure of the Spirit of God, but every man has a degree of the Holy Spirit in his life. It is the Spirit in your life that gives you faith in God, that makes you a blessing to other people. It is the Holy Spirit that is out-breathed in your soul that touches another soul and moves them for God. Begin right where you are and let God take you along the Christian life as far as you like.

Verse 10: "When Jesus heard it, He marvelled and said to them that followed, 'Verily, I say unto you, I have not found so great faith, no, not in Israel.'"

Jesus always commended faith when He met it. Jesus did not always meet faith. All the people who came to Jesus did not possess that order of faith. They had faith that if they got to Jesus they would be healed. But here is a man who says, "Speak the word only, and my servant shall be healed."

Then you remember the case of the man at the pool of Bethesda. He did not even ask to be healed. As he lay there Jesus walked up to him and said, "Wilt thou be made whole?" The poor fellow went on to say that when the water was troubled he had no one to put him in, but while waiting another stepped in ahead of him. But Jesus said unto him, "Arise, take up thy bed and walk," He was made whole. Afterward Jesus met him and said, "Behold thou art made whole: sin no more, lest a worse thing come unto thee." (John 5:14).

Most of sickness is the result of sin. That is the answer

to the individual who sins. For thousands of years men have been sinning, and in consequence of their sin, they are diseased in their bodies. This will give you an idea. Scientists tell us there are tubercular germs in 90% of the population. The only difference is that when people are in a healthy state, the germs do not get a chance to manifest themselves. I am trying to show the intimacy between sin and sickness. Not necessarily the sin of the individual. It may never be the sin of the individual.

In the records of the Lake and Graham family away back, tuberculosis was never known to them, until it appeared in my sister. My sister accompanied me to Africa and she became so ill that when I got to Cape Town we had to wait until her strength returned. God healed her.

Regarding people being healed at a distance, we receive telegrams from all over the world. Distance is no barrier to God. The United States has just finished the building of the greatest wireless station in the world. They send messages that register almost instantly, ten thousand miles away. Well, all right, when your heart strikes God in faith, it will register there wherever that individual is just that quick. All the discoveries of later years such as telegraph, telephone wireless and that sort of thing are just the common laws that Christians have practiced all their lives.

Nobody ever knelt down and prayed, but that the instant they touched God their soul registered in Jesus Christ in glory, and the answer came back to the soul. Christians have that experience every day. The wise world has begun to observe that these laws are applicable in the natural realm. I asked Marconi once how he got his first idea for the wireless, He replied he got it from watching an exhibition of telepathy in a cheap theatre.

The prayer of the heart reaches God. Jesus replied to the leper, "I will: be thou clean," The next was the centurion's servant. The centurion said "You do not need to come to my house. You speak the word only and my servant shall be healed." And in the soul of Jesus He said,

## DIVINE HEALING: A GIFT FROM GOD

"Be healed." Distance is no barrier to God. Distance makes no difference. The Spirit of God will go as far as your love reaches. Love is the medium that conveys the Spirit of God to another soul anywhere on God's earth.

This is what takes place when you pray, The Spirit of God comes upon you and bathes your soul, and a shaft of it reaches out and touches that soul over there, If you had an instrument that was fine enough to photograph spirit, you would discover this is done.

Is it not a marvellous thing that God has chosen us to be co-labourers with Him, and He takes us into partnership to do all that He is doing? Jesus Christ at the throne of God desires the blessing of you and me, and out of His holy heart the Spirit comes, and the soul is filled, and we cannot tell how or why.

I have known thousands of people to be healed who have never seen my face. They send a request for prayer, we pray, and never hear anything more about them sometimes, unless a friend or a neighbour or someone comes and tells us about them. Sometimes someone sends in a request for them. They will tell you they do not know what happened. They just got well. But you know why. That is the wonderful power that is in the Christian life, and that is the wonderful cooperation that the Lord Jesus has arranged between His own soul and the soul of the Christian. That is the Church which is his body."

JOHN G LAKE

## CHAPTER 6

# THE TRUTH ABOUT DIVINE HEALING

---

CHAPMAN SAID, JUST BEFORE HIS PASSING, "I believe the gift of healing is a far greater divine attainment than the gift of the evangelist." No wonder professor A. B. Bruce said in his Miraculous Elements of the Gospel, "Cures should be as common as conversion, and Christ's healing miracles are signs that disease does not belong to the true order of nature and are but a prophecy that the true order must be restored to us."

There is no question but what there is a universal longing for such a faith for the healing and quickening of our mortal bodies as this. Professor Bruce well expressed it in his Union Seminary lectures, which have been a power ever since their utterance:

What missionary would not be glad to be endowed with power to heal diseases as conferred by Jesus Christ on His disciples when He sent them on their Galilean mission? I know the feeling well. I spent part of my apprenticeship as a preacher and a missionary in a once prosperous but now decaying village in the west of Scotland, filled with an impoverished and exceptionally disease-stricken population. There I daily saw sights which awakened at once intense sympathy and involuntary loathing.

There were cases of cancer; strange and demoniac-like forms of insanity; children in arms, twenty years old, with the face of a full-grown man and a body not larger than an infant's. I returned home oftime sick at heart and unable to take food.

What would I not have given to have had for an hour the charisma of the Galilean evangelists! And how gladly would I have gone that day not to speak the accustomed words about a Father in heaven ever ready to receive His prodigal children, but to put an end to pain, raise the dying, and to restore to soundness shattered reason. Or had I found someday, on visiting the suffering, that they had been healed, according to their report, in answer to the prayer of some saintly friend. I should have been too thankful to have been at all skeptical. I should then have seen how He Himself took our infirmities and bore our sicknesses, and we were to represent God whose supreme purpose is, as Jesus so clearly showed, to forgive all our sins and heal all our diseases.

The place of the gift of healing in the great message of Jesus' full and complete salvation has been voiced in prophetic foregleams all through the Christian centuries, as truly as the coming Messiah by the mouth of the prophets before the appearance of Jesus.

During recent years, it has broken forth in many quarters with most unusual power. As far back as 1884, Rev. R. F. Stanton, DD, a leading Presbyterian clergyman who at one time was moderator of the general assembly of the Presbyterian church, wrote in a little volume entitled Gospel Parallelisms these remarkable words:

> It is my aim to show that the Atonement of Christ lays the foundation equally for deliverance from sin and deliverance from disease; that complete provision has been made for both; that in the exercise of faith under the conditions prescribed, we have the same reason to believe that the body may be delivered from sickness as we have the soul may be delivered from sin; in short, that both branches of the deliverance stand on the same ground and that it is necessary to include both in any true conception of what the Gospel offers to mankind.

The atoning sacrifice of Christ covers the physical as well as the spiritual needs of the race.

## COLLEGES LAG IN SCIENCE TEACHINGS

Dr. John G. Lake defined the major branches of learning as follows:

- Physiology is the science of the body.
- Psychology is the science of the soul.
- Pneumatology is the science of the spirit.
- Ontology is the science of being.

Our schools and universities teach physiology: the laws, direction, and care of the body. In the past thirty years, psychology has found recognition so that not only the universities teach this science, but lectures on psychology are in every city and hamlet. Even business houses now give psychological courses for their employees and salesmen. Yet the psyche of man will die, and the soul is mortal. Psychology is a natural science.

What are the facts of pneumatology? Firstly, that man is triune in his nature and structure—spirit, soul, and body. Secondly, that the spirit and soul are divisible. On this question, the Bible says concerning the Word of God: "Piercing even to the dividing asunder of soul and spirit" (Hebrews 4:12).

Psychology—soul science—says that the soul is the seat of the affections, desires, and emotions; the active will, the self. "My soul," said Jesus, "is exceeding sorrowful" (Matthew 26:38). "And Mary said, My soul [self] doth magnify the Lord, and my spirit hath rejoiced in God my Saviour" (Luke 1:46–47).

A type of semi-scholarship, represented by modern material scientists, has despised the Bible. No university in the United States is sufficiently advanced in scholarship to possess a chair of pneumatology.

The apostle Paul at Ephesus was received into the school of Tyrannus, a school of the Grecian philosophies. Psychology was the basis of their philosophy. Tyrannus recognized Paul's knowledge of pneumatology, the higher science, and established a chair of pneumatology. There, Paul taught the Christian philosophy, pneumatology, and psychology as Christian doctrine and experience. This resulted in the establishing of the Christian churches of Ephesus with 100,000 members. It resulted in the appointment of Timothy as the first Christian Bishop of Ephesus.

An outcome of this teaching in the school of Tyrannus was that the Grecian philosophies were discarded for the higher teaching of Christianity. From this school came Thekla, a Grecian noblewoman, a God-anointed healer, whose ministry of healing is said by students to have set a record.

And still there are those who would deny the right of Christian ministry to women.

The revelation of Jesus Christ as Savior and Healer through the simple teaching of the cross surpassed in Paul's estimation every other knowledge and led him to declare:

> I determined not to know any thing among you, save Jesus Christ, and him crucified. (1 Corinthians 2:2)

> Christ the power of God, and the wisdom of God. (1 Corinthians 1:24)

> I am not ashamed of the gospel of Christ: for it is the power of God unto salvation to every one that believeth, to the Jew first, and also to the Greek.(Romans 1:16)

Who has authority to pray for the sick? Is this holy ministry only given to the few? Is it a ministry to all Christians or to the clergy only? Jesus said:

> If ye shall ask any thing in my name, I will do it. (John 14:14)

> Ask, it shall be given you; seek, and ye shall find; knock, and it shall be opened unto you. (Luke 11:9)

> These signs shall follow them that believe; In my name shall they [believers] cast out devils; they shall speak with new tongues;…they shall lay hands on the sick, and they shall recover. (Mark 16:17–18)

The apostles were commanded to go into all the world—to make believers in every section. The signs were to follow the believers, not the apostles only.

This was heaven's characteristic. It was the trademark of the Christ on His goods. It was the brand, the stamp burned into the soul of the believer with heavenly fire.

Baptism in the Spirit of Jesus was Christ reproducing Himself in the believer: To what extent was this reproduction to be a fact? We contend that Jesus taught that the believer was empowered by the Spirit's incoming and indwelling so that he was Christ's ambassador on earth. Then he must perform Christ's most holy ministries to the sinful and sick just as Jesus himself would do.

If this is true, then the believer is a priest in every respect. The believer must then perform Christ's priestly ministry.

The believer, then, is expected to heal the sick. Jesus said that a believer should lay his hands on the sick and heal them—they were not to die; they were to recover. They were healed through the believer by the power supplied from heaven by Jesus Christ to the believer.

We desire to ask, "Should the believer-priest also forgive sins or pronounce absolution to the penitent seeker after God?" We believe he should. We are sure that it is the privilege of the modern church to see this tremendous truth that was purposed by the Lord to be the glory of Christianity.

Jesus said the believer should cast out devils. He believes he should. He does it. The devil is ejected from further possession.

How did he do it? By the exercise of the bestowed power as Christ's believer-priest, he exercises spiritual authority over the devil in the candidate and frees him from control.

In this, he has performed the Christ-function. The sick likewise are healed through the believer-priest. In this also he performs another Christ-ministry. Then how about sin?

Why does not the believer-priest by the same spiritual power and authority destroy the consciousness of sin in the soul and pronounce absolution for sins that are past?

We are asking these questions in order to discover what the believer's ministry as Christ's representative is.

We are not alone in our faith that the believer should perform the full ministry of the Christ:

"I am a priest."—Robert Browning

"The early church lost its power when it lost sight of its high priestly office."—Bishop Burnett

"The church needs to realize in new ways the inherent priesthood of Christian believers."—Lambeth Conference of Anglican Bishops, 1906

"The authority to pronounce absolution and remission of sins that are past and fulfill the aspirations of the soul for the future, I believe to be spiritual and not ecclesiastical and traditional, and to belong equally to everyone who has received such absolution and remission, and such gifts of the spiritual life." —Lyman Abbott (1835–1922)

"The experience of the Free Church confirms what we should expect from study of the New Testament and modern psychology, that the priesthood of all believers rests on sounder evidence than the priesthood of some believers."—Rev. Dr. Glover of Cambridge

"With the Quaker it is not that there is no clergy, but that there is no laity, for we are all priests unto the Highest."—John H. Graham in The Faith of the Quaker

> "I am ever in the presence not only of a Great Power, or a Great Lawgiver, but a Great Healer."—Lyman Abbott

Therefore, every believer on Jesus Christ is authorized by the Lord to do as He has done, assured of Christ's assistance:

> Greater works than these shall [ye] do, because I [Jesus] go unto my Father. (John 14:12)

> And they went forth, and preached every where, the Lord working with them, and confirming the word with signs following. (Mark 16:20)

> Lo, I am with you alway, even unto the end of the world. (Matthew 28:20)

The miracles of Jesus have been the battleground of the centuries. Men have devoted their lives in an endeavor to break down faith in miracles. Yet more believe in miracles today than ever before.

Pseudoscience declares miracles impossible. Yet the biggest men in the scientific world are believers in the supernatural and know that miracles are the discovery and utilization of which the material scientist knows nothing.

The miracle realm is man's natural realm. He is by creation the companion of the miracle-working God. Sin dethroned man from the miracle-working realm, but through grace he is coming into his own.

It has been hard for us to grasp the principles of this life of faith. In the beginning, man's spirit was the dominant force in the world; when he sinned, his mind became dominant. Sin dethroned the spirit and crowned the intellect. But grace is restoring the spirit to its place of dominion, and when man comes to realize this, he will live in the realm of the supernatural without effort. No longer will faith be a struggle but a normal living in the realm of God. The spiritual realm places men where communion with God is a normal experience.

Miracles are then his native breath. No one knows to what extent the mind and the spirit can be developed. This is not the power of mind over matter, but the power of the spirit over both mind and matter. If the body is kept in fine fettle, there is almost no limitation to man's development.

We have been slow to come to a realization that man is a spirit and that his spirit nature is his basic nature. We have sought to educate him along intellectual lines, utterly ignoring the spiritual, so man has become a self-centered, self-seeking being.

Man has lost his sense of relationship and responsibility toward God and man. That makes him lawless. We cannot ignore the spiritual side of man without magnifying the intellectual and physical; to do this without the restraint of the spirit is to unleash sin and give it dominance over the whole man.

There must be a culture and development of the spiritual nature to a point where it can enjoy fellowship with the Father God. It is above mind as God is above nature.

Man's intellect is ever conscious of supernatural forces that he cannot understand. He senses the spirit realm and longs for its freedom and creative power, but cannot enter until changed from self and sin; the spirit must be enthroned and in action rather than the intellect—spirit above both mind and matter.

## GOD DESTROYS SIN—SIN IS DEATH

Does God always heal? "In him is no darkness at all" (1 John 1:5). Can darkness come out of light? Can sickness come out of health? Is death born of life?

The issue resolves itself into this: Of what is the redemption of Jesus Christ constituted? What existing powers does He promise to destroy?

First, sin. When Christ's redemption is completed, sin is gone. "By one man sin entered into the world, and death by sin" (Romans 5:12). Death entered into the world through sin.

## SICKNESS IS INCIPIENT DEATH, DEATH IN PROCESS

Jesus "went about doing good, and healing all that were oppressed of the devil" (Acts 10:38). In Luke chapter thirteen, Jesus demanded His right to heal the woman bowed together with the spirit of infirmity as follows:

> "And ought not this woman, being a daughter of Abraham, whom Satan hath bound, lo, these eighteen years, be loosed from this bond [be healed] on the sabbath day?" (Luke 13:16); and overriding traditions of the Jews, He healed her then and there.

> The last enemy that shall be destroyed is death. (1 Corinthians 15:26)

> For this purpose the Son of God was manifested, that he might destroy the works of the devil. (1 John 3:8)

Sin, sickness, and death are doomed, doomed to death by the decree of Christ Jesus. Sin, sickness, and death are the devil's triumvirate—the triple curse.

Heaven is the absence of this triple curse; heaven is sinlessness, sicklessness, and deathlessness. This is the ultimate of Christ's redemption.

Dr. Frank N. Riale, field secretary for the Presbyterian department of education, is the author of one of the greatest books of the century, The Antidote for Sin, Sickness, and Death:

> Today, science labors to eliminate sickness and declares, "There is no reason why men should die." Science declares men are so constructed as to be perpetually renewed. Many great scientists declare the elimination of sickness to be their final objective.

Jesus anticipated the world's need. He commanded His power for the use of mankind and invites us to help ourselves to His eternal quality and become, thereby, sons of God.

## THE LOVE OF JESUS HEALED THE SICK, AFFLICTED. TAKE THE SHACKLES OFF GOD.

Jesus did not heal the sick in order to coax them to be Christians. He healed because it was His nature to heal. The multitude surrounded Him. His love gushed forth like an electric billow. "There went virtue out of him, and healed them all" (Luke 6:19).

Some modern evangelists have degraded divine healing by making it a teaser to bring those desirous of healing under the sway of their ministry. Jesus healed both saint and sinner—to the dismay of His apostles, who had not yet grown to the soul stature of Jesus. They reported to Jesus:

> "We saw one casting out devils in thy name, and he followeth not us: and we forbad him, because he followeth not us." But Jesus said,

"Forbid him not, for there is no man which shall do a miracle in my name, that can lightly speak evil of me." (Mark 9:38–39)

He met a man at the pool of Bethesda, a paralytic. This man did not ask for healing. Jesus went to him and said: "Wilt thou be made whole?" (John 5:6). Here Jesus was asking for the privilege of healing the sufferer. He healed him. His love compelled it.

Later, Jesus met the healed man in the temple and said: "Behold, thou art made whole: sin no more, lest a worse thing come unto thee" (John 5:14).

Jesus' action is a perpetual rebuke to the priestcraft who endeavor to use the possibility of the individual's healing as a means to force him into the church.

The outgushing of His love for the world burst all bounds, and four times He healed multitudes. But some say: "This was Jesus. No apostle had such an experience."

When Peter went down the street as the evening shadows fell, when his shadow reached across the street, "they brought forth the sick into the streets, and laid them on beds and couches, that at the least the shadow of Peter passing by might overshadow some of them" (Acts 5:15). The clear inference is that they were healed.

James, writing to the twelve tribes scattered abroad—not the little group of Jews constituting the kingdom of the Jews, but the whole body of the nation of Israel scattered throughout the world, both the ten-tribed kingdom and the two-tribed kingdom—shouts: "Is any sick among you? Let him call for the elders of the church; and let them pray over him"—not prepare him for death—but that "if he have committed sins, they shall be forgiven him" (James 5:14–15). He is coming into His own.

Healing was the evidence of God's forgiveness, heaven's testimony that their sins were remembered no more.

Take the shackles off God. Enlarge your theologies to Christ's standard, and the world will love and worship Him forever.

## JESUS' HEALINGS WERE NOT ALWAYS INSTANT. FAITH IS A LARGE FACTOR IN REGAINING HEALTH

In one of the letters received from readers, this question is asked: "Why are not all persons healed instantly, as Jesus healed?"

The writer of this letter is mistaken in thinking that Jesus always healed instantly. A case in point is the healing of the ten lepers; as they went, they were cleansed. (See Luke 17:14.) The healing virtue was administered. The healing process became evident later.

Again, Jesus laid His hands on a blind man and then inquired, "What do you see?" The man replied, "I see men as walking trees." His sight was still imperfect. Then Jesus laid His hands on him the second time and he saw clearly. (See Mark 8:23–25.)

Healing is by degree, based on two conditions: first, the degree of healing virtue administered; second, the degree of faith that gives action and power to the virtue administered.

The word preached did not profit them, not being mixed with faith in them that heard it. (Hebrews 4:2)

## GOD PASSES ON POWERS
## TO CURE TO ALL FOLLOWERS

Jesus not only healed the sick, but performed a creative miracle on the man born blind. (See John 9.) Being born blind, it is self-evident the eyes were not a finished creation. Otherwise, he would have seen. The narrative reveals that the blind man did not know who Jesus was. Jesus did not make Himself known until after the miracle had been performed. Let us analyze the incident.

Jesus discovered the man born blind. (See verse 1.) He then spat on the ground and made clay of the spittle. Why? Because Jesus was a fundamentalist. The story of creation in Genesis says that "God formed man of the dust of the ground" (Genesis 2:7). Jesus, in finishing the creation of the eyes, adopted the same method. He stooped down, took up some dust, spat on it, and put it on the blind man. This was not healing. It was a work of creation.

In 1 Corinthians, the twelfth chapter, it is said that in distributing the gifts of the Spirit to the members of the church, one was given the "gifts of healing...[and] to another the working of miracles" (1 Corinthians 12:9–10). Healing is the renewal of the body from diseased conditions. A miracle is in the creative order. The case of the blind man was an exercise of creative authority, not the restoration of diseased tissue. The man was made whole.

The grouchers made their kick. The Pharisees examined the man and asked, "Who healed you?"

He answered, "I know not" (John 9:12).

It is clearly evident to students of divine healing that sometimes the Spirit of God is ministered to the sick person to a degree that he is manifestly supercharged with the Spirit. Just as a person holds a galvanic battery until the system is charged with electric force, yet no real and final healing takes place until something occurs that releases the faith of the individual, a flash of divine power is observed, a veritable explosion has taken place in the sick person, and the disease is destroyed.

This tangibility of the Spirit of God is the scientific secret of healing.

A diseased woman followed Jesus in a crowd. She knew the law of the Spirit and had observed that it flowed from the person of Jesus and healed the sick. She was convinced it must also be present in His clothing. So she reasoned: "If I could but touch the hem of His garment, I would be made whole." (See Mark 5:28; Matthew 9:20–21.) She did so. She was healed of a twelve-year sickness that had baffled physicians and left her in poverty.

Jesus was aware that someone had been healed. He turned to ask who it was. Peter said, "See how the multitude is thronging and jostling You."

But Jesus answered, "Someone has touched Me, for I perceive that virtue has gone out of Me." Jesus was aware of the outflow.

The woman was aware of the reception. Her healing was a fact. (See Mark 5:25–34.) Here, faith and the power of God were apparent. It was a veritable chemical reaction. Healing always is.

I believe the reason that people do not see the possibilities of divine healing is that they are not aware of its scientific aspects. The grace and love of God in the soul opens the nature to God. The Spirit of God resounds.

When the Pharisees asked the man who had been born blind, "What do you think of Him?" he replied, "He is a prophet" (John 9:17).

Later, Jesus found him and said to him, "Dost thou believe on the Son of God?" (verse 35).

The man replied, "Who is he, Lord, that I might believe on him?" (verse 36).

Jesus answered, "I that speak unto thee am he." (Verse 37.)

The struggle of the centuries has been to free the soul of man from narrow interpretations. Jesus has sometimes been made to appear as a little bigot, sometimes as an impostor. The world is still waiting to see Him as He is: Jesus the magnificent, Jesus the giant, Jesus the compassionate, Jesus the dynamic—the wonder of the centuries.

Take the shackles off God. Let Him have a chance to bless mankind without ecclesiastical limitations.

As a missionary, I have witnessed the healing of

thousands of heathens. Thus was Christ's love and compassion for a lost world revealed. And thus, the writer was assisted into the larger vision of a world-redeemer whose hand and heart are extended to God's big world, and every man—saint and sinner—is invited to behold and love Him.

## JESUS USED SCIENCE TO HEAL THE AFFLICTED

The law of contact and transmission was the medium through which the master wrought miracles.

Mrs. John W. Goudy of Chicago writes, "How can you speak of divine healing as scientific if healing is through the atonement of Jesus Christ? How can the matter of atonement and grace be considered scientific?"

Atonement through the grace of God is scientific in its application. Jesus used many methods of healing the sick. All were scientific. Science is the discovery of how God does things.

Jesus laid His hands upon the sick in obedience to the law of contact and transmission. Contact of His hands with the sick one permitted the Spirit of God in Him to flow into the sick man.

The sick woman who touched His clothes found that the Spirit emanated from His person. She touched the "hem of His garment" and the Spirit flashed into her. She was made whole (See Mark 5:27–29.) This was a scientific process.

Paul, knowing this law, laid his hands upon handkerchiefs and aprons. The Bible says that when they were laid upon the sick, they were healed, and the demons went out of those possessed. Materialists have said this was superstition. It is entirely scientific. The Spirit of God emanating from Paul transformed the handkerchiefs into "storage batteries" of Holy Spirit power. When they were laid upon the sick, they surcharged the body, and healing was the result (See Acts 19:12.)

This demonstrates, firstly, that the Spirit of God is a tangible substance, a heavenly materiality. Secondly, it is capable of being stored in the substance of a handkerchief, as demonstrated in the garments of Jesus or in the handkerchiefs of Paul. Thirdly, it will transmit power from handkerchiefs to the sick person. Fourthly, its action in the sick man was so powerful that the disease departed. Fifthly, the demonized also were relieved. Both the sick and insane were healed by this method.

While the scientific mind always asks "how" and "why," it is not necessary for the soul desiring Christ's blessing to have any knowledge of the scientific process by which healing or salvation is accomplished.

Jesus said, "He that receiveth me" (Matthew 10:40; John 13:20). Men receive Jesus Christ into the heart as one receives a lover. It is an affectionate relationship. Men obey Him because they love Him. They obey Him because they have received Him affectionately. He has become their souls' lover.

His love and power in them redeems them from sin and sickness and eventually, we are promised in His Word, He will also redeem us from death. Redemption from sin, sickness, and death constitutes man's deliverance from bondage to Satan and his kingdom (see Hosea 13:14), and establishes the kingdom of heaven.

## THE BIBLE SHOWS JESUS HEALED THE SICK BY HIS WORD. EXERCISED AUTHORITY OVER DISEASE BY SPEAKING TO THOSE AFFLICTED

Yesterday we discussed Jesus healing through the laying on of hands. Today we will examine Jesus healing by the word command, and other methods.

They brought to him a man sick of the palsy, lying on a bed, and Jesus seeing their faith [the faith of those who brought the man as well as that of the man himself] said unto the sick of the palsy, "Son, be of good cheer; thy sins be forgiven thee." (Matthew 9:2)

The scribes thought to themselves, "This man [Jesus] blasphemeth" (verse 3). Jesus met this opposition by saying,

> Wherefore think ye evil in your hearts? For whether is easier, to say, "Thy sins be forgiven thee"; or to say, "Arise, and walk?" But that ye may know that the Son of man hath power on earth to forgive sins, (then saith he to the sick of the palsy,) Arise, take up thy bed, and go unto thine house. (Matthew 9:4–6)

The man arose and walked. No hands were laid on this man. There was no external ministry of any kind. Jesus commanded; the man was healed.

They brought a man who was dumb [mute], possessed of a devil. When the devil was cast out, the man spoke. The people wondered. This also is His exercise of spiritual authority (See Matthew 9:32–33.) When Jesus commanded, the power of God entered and ejected the demon.

At Capernaum a centurion came saying, "Lord, my servant lieth at home sick of the palsy, grievously tormented." Jesus said, "I will come and heal him." The centurion answered, "Not so. Speak the word only, and my servant shall be healed. That is enough." And Jesus said, "Go home. It is done." The record shows the servant was healed. (See Matthew 8:6–8, 13.)

Many have laughed at the idea of man being healed long distances from the one who ministers in Jesus' name. But here is a clear case, and the God-anointed may still command God's power. To the needy, distance is no barrier.

I now present mass healing. Four times it is recorded in the Gospels that "He healed multitudes; there went out a virtue from Him, and He healed them all." There was no personal touch. (See Matthew 12:15, 14:14, 15:30, 19:2.)

God is not confined to methods. Heaven bows to the soul with faith anywhere, under any conditions. "Whosoever will, let him take of the water of life freely" (Revelation 22:17).

Again, Jesus said, "If two of you shall agree on earth as touching any thing that they shall ask, it shall be done for them" (Matthew 18:19).

"Hitherto have ye asked nothing in my name: ask, and ye shall receive, that your joy may be full" (John 16:24), said Jesus.

The apostle James gave command that elders of the church should pray for the sick and anoint them with oil. Oil is the symbol of the healing Spirit. This is a command: "Pray for the sick that they may be healed." (See James 5:14–15.)

Where? Anywhere.

When? Forever. As long as Jesus Christ reigns in heaven. As long as men on earth have faith in Him.

The voice of Jesus still is heard saying, "Whatsoever ye shall ask in my name, that will I do" (John 14:13).

"Ask, seek, knock—find Jesus." (See Matthew 7:7–8; Luke 11:9–10.)

"With God all things are possible" (Mark 10:27), and "all things are possible to him that believeth" (Mark 9:23).

Divine healing through prayer is as old as the race of man. The first book of the Bible, Genesis, records the healing of the wives of a heathen king in response to the prayer of Abraham. (See Genesis 20:17.)

The second book of the Bible, Exodus, gives us the terms of a distinctive covenant between the nation of Israel and Jehovah Rapha, "The Lord thy Healer." In this covenant God not only agreed to heal the people when sick, but not to permit the sicknesses of Egypt to touch them. Its terms are:

> If thou wilt diligently hearken to the voice of the Lord thy God, and wilt do that which is right in his sight, and wilt give ear to his commandments, and keep all his statutes [on this condition, Jehovah agrees], I will put none of these diseases upon thee, which I have brought upon the Egyptians: for I am the Lord that healeth thee. (Exodus 15:26)

Under this covenant, the twelve-tribed nation lived without doctors or medicine for 450 years, until the nation of Israel had an army of 1,100,000, and Judah an army of 500,000. Figuring on the same basis as the number of Americans in the army during the world war, this would give Israel and Judah a combined population of between 25,000,000 and 30,000,000.

King David of Israel gave the most extraordinary health report that history records: he said, "There was not one feeble person among their tribes" (Psalm 105:37).

Such historic data should go far to convince the world of our day that an absolute trust in God is not only a safe policy, but a most scientific guarantee of national health.

In this connection we must examine Israel's national constitution as it was made the basis of national health. Firstly, its basic principles were the Ten Commandments. Secondly, it contained a law in which Jehovah held perpetual title to the land. Thirdly, a credit and mortgage statute. Fourthly, a distribution of surplus wealth statute. Fifthly, the most extraordinary labor law ever written. Sixthly, an absolutely equitable tax law by which every citizen paid one-tenth of his increase. (See Deuteronomy 5–26.)

This is the only national constitution given directly by Jehovah and is the foundation of all national constitutions.

For keeping this constitution, Jehovah guaranteed the nation against wars, pestilences, poverty, destructive droughts, and lastly, "I will take sickness away from the midst of thee." (See Deuteronomy 7:15.)

The broad scope of divine healing in Israel is the basis of all faith in God for healing and was the foundation of the ministry of Jesus Christ, Israel's Redeemer and the world's Savior.

Israel had been kept free of disease for 450 years through divine healing. Outside of Israel there was no divine healing. No other religion in the world possessed healing power. There is not a single instance of this power in the life of India, Egypt, China, or Africa.

The Hebrews alone, from Abraham onward, exhibited the power of healing at this time. Later, knowledge of Israel's God and His power to heal disease spread through the nations of the world.

The prophets of Israel were marvelous men of God. At their word, empires rose and fell. Life and death obeyed their will. Earth and sky answered their call. Before their eyes, future history marched with events of the present. No men of any other nation equaled them. No bibliotheca of any other nation compared with their Holy Scriptures.

## CHRIST, GOD'S GIFT

Christ came as God's gift to Israel and Israel only. To Judah, the remnant of Israel, He came. Despite all that has been imagined and written of miracles in His childhood, there is not a particle of evidence that He performed any miracles until, at Cana of Galilee, He turned water into wine. The Bible states this miracle was the beginning of miracles by Jesus. (See John 2:1–11.)

Jesus performed no public ministry until He was thirty. The law of Moses forbade it. So we read that when Jesus was about thirty, He came to John the Baptist and was baptized. (See 1 Chronicles 23:3 and Luke 3:21–23.)

His baptism was His dedication of Himself to the heavenly Father. He dedicated body, soul, and spirit. To

John, He said, "Into all righteousness." (See Matthew 3:15.)

He was dedicating Himself to God to reveal the righteousness of God. Jesus' dedication was wholly unselfish. But His dedication in itself was not sufficient to qualify Him to reveal God. His humanity must be submerged in the Holy Spirit. As He was baptized in Jordan, this took place.

Now He must be tested. He was led of the Holy Spirit into the wilderness to be tempted by Satan. This was to find if His dedication was a fact or if He would fail under the forty-day test.

Three temptations were applied. Firstly, a psychological temptation to His mind—love of acclaim. Secondly, a spiritual temptation applied to His spirit—that He might by a simple acknowledgment of Satan secure "all the kingdoms of the world" (Matthew 4:8).

When He conquered, the natural result took place in Himself. Having overcome, the consciousness of inherent power was radiant in Him. "And Jesus returned in the power of the Spirit" (Luke 4:14). (See Matthew 4:1–11 and Luke 4:1–13.)

Jesus now makes the next advance; He proclaims His platform. Returning to Nazareth, He boldly declares, "The Spirit of the Lord is upon me. (1) He has anointed me to preach the gospel to the poor; (2) He has sent me to heal the brokenhearted; (3) to proclaim liberty to the captive; (4) recovering of sight to the blind; (5) to set at liberty them that are bruised; (6) to preach the acceptable year of the Lord." (See Luke 4:18–19.)

No more waiting for the release of the year of Jubilee. Jesus Christ, the Eternal Jubilee, was at hand to save and heal.

Jesus' ministry of healing and the marvelous faith in God that He exhibited in miracle working were no accident. Miracles must be His very breath, for 800 years before His birth the prophet Isaiah had proclaimed:

He will come and save you. Then the eyes of the blind shall be opened, and the ears of the deaf shall be unstopped. Then shall the lame man leap as an hart, and the tongue of the dumb sing. (Isaiah 35:4–6)

So to be Savior of the world, He must be forever the miracle-worker of the ages; the death destroyer; the finality of revelation of the majesty, power, and mercy of Jesus!

The very name was a miracle.
The angel announced it.
Jesus' birth was a miracle.
His wisdom was a miracle.
His life was a miracle.
His teachings were miraculous.
He lived and walked in the realm of the miraculous.
He made miracles common.
His death was a miracle.
His resurrection was a miracle.
His appearances after death were miraculous.
His ascension was a staggering miracle.

His pouring out of the Spirit on the day of Pentecost was the outstanding miracle. It was the one event in which His whole Saviorhood climaxed. Out of heaven was given to His followers the Spirit of the Eternal, to do in them all it had done in Him. Sin, sickness, and death were doomed.

He came as a roaring tempest, as tongues of fire crowning the one hundred and twenty as the living eternal Spirit entering into them. He proclaimed His triumphant entry into man through speaking in languages they knew not.

HIS DEITY HAD LIFTED THEM INTO HIS REALM,

## TRANSFIGURED, TRANSFORMED, TRANSMUTED

Jesus bestowed the power to heal upon His disciples:

> Then he called his twelve disciples together, and gave them power and authority over all devils, and to cure diseases. And he sent them to preach the kingdom of God, and to heal the sick....And they departed, and went through the towns, preaching the gospel, and healing every where. (Luke 9:1–2, 6)

He likewise bestowed power to heal upon the seventy:

> After these things the Lord appointed other seventy also, and sent them two and two before his face into every city and place, whither he himself would come....Heal the sick that are therein, and say unto them, The kingdom of God is come nigh unto you. (Luke 10:1, 9)

In order to be fully informed on the question of divine healing, let us study this question as part of the fully-rounded development and life of Jesus.

In beginning His revelation of the life of God for, and in, man, Jesus chose the order of nature as the realm of His first demonstration. (1) Jesus turned the water into wine. (See John 2:1–10.) (2) He stifled the waves (See Luke 8:24). (3) He walked on water (See Matthew 14:25). These revelations of power over nature each surpassed the other.

Then Jesus astounded His followers by turning to the creative life of God. He fed the multitude by an act of creative power when He created fish and bread to feed five thousand. (See Matthew 14:15–21).

This shows the distinction between healings and miracles. Miracles are creative. Healing is a restoration of what has been.

## DIVINE HEALING: A GIFT FROM GOD

Jesus now advances into a new sphere, the order of sickness. Here He meets the mind of the other that must be conformed to His. (1) Jesus heals Peter's wife's mother. This is first degree healing (See Matthew 8:14–15). (2) Jesus meets the blind man and heals him. This is second degree healing (See Mark 8:22–26). (3) The lepers are healed—healing in the third degree. (See Luke 17:11–19).

Again, Jesus enters the creative realm and creates eyes in a man born blind. Blindness from birth is evidence of an unfinished condition of the eyes. The creative process was not complete. Jesus stooped, took dust from the road, spat upon it, and put it on the man's eyes. In so doing, He finished a work of creation; the man saw (See John 9:1–7).

Now, Jesus again advances. This time He chooses the order of death. (1) He raised the daughter of Jarius, dead a few minutes. This is the first degree (See Mark 5:22–24, 38–42). (2) Jesus meets a funeral procession coming out of the city of Nain. He commands the young man to live, and he sat up. This man was dead many hours. This is the second degree (See Luke 7:11–15). (3) His friend Lazarus is dead four days. His body is in a state of decomposition. Jesus commands Lazarus to come forth. He who was dead arose. This was the third degree (See John 11:1–15).

Now, Jesus again steps into the creative realm and announces His coming death. He declares of His life, "I have power to lay it down, and I have power to take it again" (John 10:18).

Through this chain of successive abandonment to God, we discover the soul-steps of Jesus. Every step was taken with reliance on the Word of God as the all-sufficient guide.

Jesus took the promises of God in the Scriptures and permitted them to work out in His soul. Therefore, His promises to us are not made on His own speculation, but because of His soul's discovery of the mind of God. But He did not let it rest there. He took each discovered promise and worked it out.

He discovered the promise of supply and fed the multitude. He discovered healing power and made the blind to see, the deaf to hear, the lame to walk. He discovered the promise of "man the master" when anointed of God, and He stilled the waves and turned the water into wine; of life ever-present, and He raised Lazarus and the widow's son; of life everlasting, and He rose Himself from the grave.

He gave His promises as discovered and demonstrated truth, and He tells us these things shall be ours as we are lifted by the Spirit into the God realm, the Christ-conscious realm.

But it is the one real thing among the myriads of life's illusions and contains in itself man's future hope and his transcendent glory. Herein is the true dominion of man.

## THE MARVELOUS EXPERIENCE OF CHRIST'S "DEATH MINISTRY" PRODUCED IN HIS SOUL THE POWER AND GLORY OF THE RESURRECTION

We have followed Jesus through the continued ascents of His earthly career. Jesus has developed in faith and knowledge and "in favour with God and man" (Luke 2:52) at every step. If we were to stop at this point and refuse to follow Him to the throne of the universe, we would miss the whole purpose of His life. Divine healing and every other outflow of His holy soul would be beggared and perverted if we failed here.

Christianity is not a mere philosophy. It is more. It is very much more. Christianity is not simply obedience to beautiful commandments. Christianity is not only the acceptance of glorious promises. Christianity is a divine content. Christianity is a heavenly dynamic. Christianity is the ultimate of all consciousness of God. Christianity is wholly supernatural. Christianity comes down from heaven from the innermost heart of the glorified Christ.

Christianity is in the innermost and uttermost of man declaring, "I am he that liveth, and was dead; and, behold, I am alive for evermore, Amen; and have the keys of hell and of death" (Revelation 1:18). Christianity is the spotless descent of God into man and the sinless ascent of man into God. The Holy Spirit is the agent by whom it is accomplished.

The significance of Jesus' death was not in His sacrifice only, but also in His achievement in the regions of death - He took death captive. He liberated those who, in death, awaited His coming and deliverance. Jesus took them in triumph from the control of the angel of death and transferred them to His own glory.

David prophesied, "He ascended upon high. He led captivity captive. He gave gifts unto men, even unto the rebellious also, that they might know the mercy of the Lord" (See Psalm 68:18).

Peter declared, "Christ went and preached unto the spirits in prison, while once the long-suffering of God waited in the days of Noah while the ark was being prepared." (See 1 Peter 3:18–20.)

And lest we fail to comprehend the source of His ministry in death, Peter says again, "For this cause was the gospel preached also to them that are dead, that they might be judged according to men in the flesh, but live according to God in the spirit" (1 Peter 4:6).

The apocryphal book of Nicodemus relates this: "Jesus came to the regions of death, released the captives, and proclaimed liberty" (See The Gospel of Nicodemus 6:1).

It was this marvelous experience of Jesus in death ministry that produced in His soul the glory-power of the resurrection, not only His personal triumph over death, but the release of those held in death's chains.

In all the universe there was none with such triumph in his spirit as Jesus possessed when death's bars were broken. With power heretofore unknown, He commanded His followers, saying, "All power is given unto me in heaven and in earth" (Matthew 28:18).

Glorifying in this amazing ascent in consciousness, He instantly found the eleven and breathed on them, saying: "Receive ye the Holy Ghost" (John 20:22). This was Jesus' endeavor to lift them into the same soul triumph that He enjoyed.

The ascension was a further advance in triumphant consciousness, climaxed by His presentation of Himself at the throne of God, where, Peter says, "He received from the Father the gift of the Holy Spirit" (See Acts 2:33). This was Jesus' divine equipment as world Savior. From then on, He was empowered to administer the transcendent glory-power to all who would receive—divine healing, saving power. The empowering of the Christian soul from on high is the pouring forth of the Holy Spirit by Jesus Christ, High Priest of heaven.

That we may realize the uttermost of ultimate transcendence of the soul of Jesus in glory, hear Him declare anew:

> I am he that liveth and was dead; and, behold, I am alive for evermore, Amen; and have the keys of hell and of death (Revelation 1:18).

Who would not rejoice to place himself in the hands of such a Savior and Physician?

Answering forever the world's questions: "Is He able to heal? Does He ever heal? Does He always heal?"—to all we boldly say, "Yes, He is Jesus, triumphant, eternal, omnipotent."

Jesus called His twelve disciples and commanded upon them power and authority to cast out devils and heal disease (See Luke 9:1). He superseded this by declaring: "If ye shall ask anything in my name…it shall be done" (John 14:14, 15:7).

The first was a limited power of attorney; the second, unlimited. This unlimited power of attorney was authorized before His crucifixion. It was to become effective when the Holy Ghost came.

On the day of Pentecost this power of attorney was made fully operative. The Spirit came. First, legally, they had His Word. Then, vitally, He sent His Spirit.

Peter and John instantly grasped the significance of the name. Passing into the temple, they met a beggar-cripple. He was forty years old and had been crippled from birth. Peter commanded, "In the name of Jesus Christ of Nazareth, rise up and walk" (Acts 3:6). Heaven's lightning struck the man. He leaped to his feet, whole.

A multitude rushed up. They demanded, "In what name, by what power, have ye done this?" Peter and John replied, "In the name of Jesus Christ of Nazareth, whom ye slew, whom God raised up" (See Acts 3:12–16). Matchless name! The secret of power was in it. When they used the name, power struck. The dynamite of heaven exploded.

Peter and John were hustled to jail. The church prayed for them in "the name." They were released. They went to the church. The entire church prayed that signs and wonders might be done. How did they pray? In "the name." They used it legally. The vital response was instantaneous. The place was shaken as by an earthquake. Tremendous name! (See Acts 3:1–16; 4:1–10, 23–31)

Jesus commanded, "Go ye into all the world" (Mark 16:15). What for? To proclaim the name; to use the name; to baptize believers. How? In the name. Amazing name! In it was concentrated the combined authority resident in the Father, the Son, and the Holy Ghost. Almighty name!

The apostles used the name. It worked. The deacons at Samaria used the name. The fire flashed. Believers everywhere, forever, were commanded to use it. The name detonated round the world.

More Bibles are sold today than any other 100 books. Why? The name is in it. It's finality—"at the name of Jesus every knee [shall] bow...and every tongue [shall] confess"

(Philippians 2:10–11).

Prayer in this name gets answers. The Moravians prayed, and the greatest revival till that time hit the world. Finney prayed, and America rocked with the power. Hudson Taylor prayed, and China's Inland Mission was born. Evan Roberts prayed for seven years, and the Welsh revival resulted.

An old Negro, Seymour of Azusa, prayed five hours a day for three-and-a-half years. He prayed seven hours a day for two-and-a-half years more. Heaven's fire fell over the world, and the most extensive revival of real religion in this century resulted.

He said unto them,

> Go ye into all the world, and preach the gospel to every creature. He that believeth and is baptized shall be saved; but he that believeth not shall be damned. And these signs shall follow them that believe; In my name shall they cast out devils; they shall speak with new tongues; they shall take up serpents; and if they drink any deadly thing, it shall not hurt them; they shall lay hands on the sick, and they shall recover. (Mark 16:15–18)

And lest healing should be lost to the church, He perpetuated it forever as one of the nine gifts of the Holy Ghost.

> To one is given by the Spirit the word of wisdom; to another the word of knowledge by the same Spirit; to another faith by the same Spirit; to another the gifts of healing by the same Spirit; to another the working of miracles; to another prophecy; to another discerning of spirits; to another divers kinds of tongues; to another the interpretation of tongues. (1 Corinthians 12:8–10)

## THE CHURCH WAS COMMANDED TO PRACTICE IT

> Is any among you afflicted? let him pray. Is any merry? let him sing psalms. Is any sick among you? let him call for the elders of the church; and let them pray over him, anointing him with oil in the name of the Lord: and the prayer of faith shall save the sick, and the Lord shall raise him up; and if he hath committed sins, they shall be forgiven him. Confess your faults one to another, and pray one for another, that ye may be healed. The effectual fervent prayer of a righteous man availeth much (James 5:13–16).

The unchangeableness of God's eternal purpose is thereby demonstrated: "Jesus Christ the same yesterday, and today, and for ever" (Hebrews 13:8), and "I am the Lord, I change not" (Malachi 3:6).

God always was the Healer. He is the Healer still and will ever remain the Healer. Healing is for you. Jesus healed all who came to Him. (See for example, Matthew 8:36; 9:35; 12:15; Luke 4:40; 6:19.) He never turned anyone away. He never said, "It is not God's will to heal you," or that it was better for the individual to remain sick or that they were being perfected in character through the sickness. He healed them all, thereby demonstrating forever God's unchangeable will concerning sickness and healing.

Have you need of healing? Pray to God in the name of Jesus Christ to remove the diseases. Command it to leave, as you would sin. Assert your divine authority and refuse to have it. Jesus purchased your freedom from sickness as He purchased your freedom from sin.

His own self bare our sins in his own body on the tree, that we, being dead to sins, should live unto righteousness:

by whose stripes ye were healed. (1 Peter 2:24)

Therefore, mankind has a right to health, as he has a right to deliverance from sin. If you do not have it, it is because you are being cheated out of your inheritance. It belongs to you. In the name of Jesus Christ, go after it and get it.

If your faith is weak, call for those who believe and to whom the prayer of faith and the ministry of healing have been committed.

Made in the USA
Middletown, DE
29 March 2025